D0528241

Sweet Old-Fashioned Favourites

Bounty Books

Introduction

The tastes we remember with most fondness and nostalgia are the sweet old-fashioned favourites of our childhood – treacle tart, lemon meringue and more. We've turned back the clock to the days of Grandma's kitchen, and compiled a selection of scrumptious puddings, bakes and sweet treats that will certainly stir some memories.

ACP Magazines Ltd and Bounty Books hereby exclude all liability to the extent permitted by law for any errors or omissions in this book and for any loss, damage or expense (whether direct or indirect) suffered by a third party relying on any information contained in this book.

This paperback edition published in 2011 by Bounty Books,
a division of Octopus Publishing Group Limited,
Endeavour House, 189 Shaftesbury Avenue, London WC2H 8JY
www.octopusbooks.co.uk

An Hachette UK Company
www.hachette.co.uk

Copyright © ACP Magazines Ltd 2008

All rights reserved. No part of this publication may be reproduced, stored in a retrieval system or transmitted by any means, electronic, mechanical, photocopying, recording or otherwise without the prior written permission of the copyright holder.

ISBN: 978-0-753722-09-1

Printed and bound in China

contents

tips & techniques

Here, we share our tips and show you the techniques that will make your cooking simple and enjoyable.

1

2

to beat egg whites

Egg whites are often beaten to 'soft peaks' or 'firm peaks'. Exercise care, because if whites are over-beaten it makes them difficult to fold through another mixture.

SOFT PEAKS

1 This picture shows soft peaks: mounds of mixture after a short time of beating at a high speed.

FIRM PEAKS

2 This picture shows firm peaks: the peaks are slightly dryer and more voluminous than soft peaks.

to separate eggs

- A recipe may specify egg yolks and whites used separately. Crack shell by tapping gently on flat surface or sharp edge, preferably not the mixing bowl; break shell in half and 'see-saw' yolk between shells to allow white to run into bowl.
- It is a good idea to break each egg separately into a cup, to ensure freshness, before adding it to other eggs.
- If a recipe requires egg white to be beaten to a fluffy stage, it is vital that not a speck of yolk goes into the white, or the white simply won't beat up. However, should this happen, use a teaspoon to remove the yolk from the white.

1

2

3

4

mixing techniques

TO RUB IN BUTTER

1 Use fingertips to rub butter through dry ingredients.

TO CREAM

2 Add essence or any flavouring to chopped butter; beat in small bowl until mixture is as white as possible. Add sugar; beat until light and fluffy. You can also use your hand or wooden spoon. Proceed as directed in individual recipes.

TO FOLD IN

3 This method of mixing is important to master; the object is to combine the ingredients as evenly, gently and quickly as possible to prevent the light mixture from deflating.

- We like to use a plastic spatula so ingredients can be easily incorporated from the base of the bowl through to the top surface of the mixture.
- Once you've achieved this folding over and over action, you won't have any trouble making sponges, soufflés or mousses, etc.

TO BLEND

4 This is the process of gradually stirring a liquid into a dry ingredient until the mixture is smooth (without lumps) and combined. This picture shows you how to blend cornflour and water together.

to melt chocolate

- Ensure the chocolate does not come into contact with the water. Therefore, never cover chocolate when melting it, as condensation can cause chocolate to 'seize' and become lumpy.
- When using a saucepan, ensure the base of the container holding the chocolate does not touch the hot water, as the heat will cause it to burn.
- For best results, melt chocolate in an uncovered, microwave-safe container on HIGH (100%) in 30-second bursts; remove immediately when melted.

to toast

Nuts and coconut can be toasted by several methods. They don't need butter, due to the presence of natural oils. After toasting, remove immediately from tray or pan to cool.

TO TOAST NUTS

1 Spread nuts on oven tray; bake in moderate oven about 5 minutes or until browned lightly.

TO TOAST COCONUT

2 Place coconut in heavy-base frying pan; stir over medium heat until coconut is browned lightly and evenly.

1

2

cakes
large & small

bread & butter pudding cake

PREPARATION TIME 40 MINUTES (PLUS STANDING TIME)
BAKING TIME 1 HOUR 20 MINUTES

55g SULTANAS
55g RAISINS
50g COARSELY CHOPPED DRIED APRICOTS
35g CURRANTS
65g CHOPPED DRIED FIGS
2 TABLESPOONS MIXED PEEL
60ml BRANDY
2 TABLESPOONS ORANGE JUICE
2 SMALL BRIOCHE (200g)
80g BUTTER, MELTED
80g APRICOT JAM, WARMED
1 TABLESPOON ICING SUGAR

SPONGE
4 EGGS
110g CASTER SUGAR
110g SELF-RAISING FLOUR
50g BUTTER, MELTED

CUSTARD
300ml WHIPPING CREAM
250ml MILK
2 EGGS
4 EGG YOLKS
110g CASTER SUGAR

1 Combine dried fruits, peel, brandy and juice in medium bowl, cover; stand overnight.
2 Preheat oven to moderately hot (200°C/180°C fan-assisted). Grease and flour deep 22cm (9in) round cake tin.
3 Make sponge. Make custard.
4 Decrease oven to moderately low (160°C/140°C fan-assisted).
5 Grease same cleaned cake tin; line base and side with baking parchment, extending paper 5cm (2in) above edge of tin. Cut each brioche vertically into six slices; brush slices on both sides with a quarter of the combined butter and jam.
6 Using serrated knife, split cake into three layers; place bottom layer in prepared tin, brush with another quarter of the jam mixture. Using 6cm (2½in) cutter, cut eight rounds from middle layer; brush rounds on both sides with another quarter of the jam mixture, reserve. Chop remaining cake layer coarsely.
7 Layer half of the brioche then fruit mixture, chopped cake and remaining brioche slices in tin. Pour over remaining jam mixture. Pour hot custard over layered ingredients; top with reserved rounds. Bake, uncovered, in moderately low oven 30 minutes. Cover with foil; bake further 30 minutes; turn, top-side up, onto serving plate. Dust with sifted icing sugar.

SPONGE Beat eggs and sugar in small bowl with electric mixer until thick and creamy; transfer to large bowl. Gently fold in triple-sifted flour and butter. Pour mixture into prepared tin; bake, uncovered, in moderately hot oven about 20 minutes. Turn cake onto wire rack immediately to cool.

CUSTARD Stir cream and milk in small saucepan over heat until almost boiling. Whisk eggs, yolks and sugar in large bowl. Whisking constantly, gradually add hot cream mixture to egg mixture; whisk until combined.

SERVES 12

TIP You can use a purchased sponge cake, if you prefer.

STORAGE Sponge can be made 1 day ahead; cover and refrigerate overnight.

TIPS The eggs should be at room temperature and the butter softened but not melted.
■ Always add any flavourings and essences in with the butter for maximum flavour.
■ Stir flour and any liquid into the mixture in 2 batches to facilitate mixing; beat in eggs, 1 at a time, after breaking separately first in a saucer to make sure they're fresh.

STORAGE Cake best made on day of serving.
■ Cake can be frozen for up to 3 months.

The mixture should be light and fluffy

victoria sandwich

Among the many memorials to Queen Victoria are several culinary creations. The Victoria sandwich is undoubtedly the best known.

PREPARATION TIME 15 MINUTES BAKING TIME 25 MINUTES

250g BUTTER
1 TEASPOON VANILLA ESSENCE
220g CASTER SUGAR
4 EGGS
300g SELF-RAISING FLOUR
2 TABLESPOONS JAM
ICING SUGAR

1 Grease 2 deep 20cm (8in) round cake tins, cover bases with baking parchment; grease paper.
2 Beat butter, essence and sugar in small bowl with electric mixer until mixture is light and fluffy. Add eggs 1 at a time, beating well after additions.
3 Transfer mixture to large bowl, stir in sifted flour in 2 batches.
4 Spread mixture evenly in prepared tins; bake in moderate oven about 25 minutes. Turn cakes onto wire rack to cool. Join cakes with jam; dust cake with a little sifted icing sugar.

SERVES 6

ginger cake

PREPARATION TIME 15 MINUTES BAKING TIME 1 HOUR 30 MINUTES

300g FIRMLY PACKED BROWN SUGAR
225g PLAIN FLOUR
225g SELF-RAISING FLOUR
½ TEASPOON BICARBONATE OF SODA
1 TABLESPOON GROUND GINGER
2 TEASPOONS GROUND CINNAMON
1 TEASPOON GROUND NUTMEG
250g BUTTER, SOFTENED
2 EGGS
250ml BUTTERMILK
175g GOLDEN SYRUP

LEMON FROSTING
60g BUTTER, SOFTENED
2 TEASPOONS FINELY GRATED LEMON RIND
2 TABLESPOONS LEMON JUICE
320g ICING SUGAR

1 Position oven shelves; preheat oven to moderately low. Grease deep 23cm (9in) square cake tin; line base with baking parchment.
2 Sift dry ingredients into large bowl of electric mixer; add remaining ingredients. Beat mixture on low speed until ingredients are combined, then beat on medium speed until mixture is smooth and changed to a paler colour. Using metal spatula, spread mixture into prepared tin.
3 Bake cake in moderately low oven about 1½ hours. Stand cake 10 minutes, turn onto wire rack, turn top-side up to cool. Spread cold cake with lemon frosting.

LEMON FROSTING Using wooden spoon, beat butter and rind together in small bowl; gradually beat in juice and icing sugar.

SERVES 24

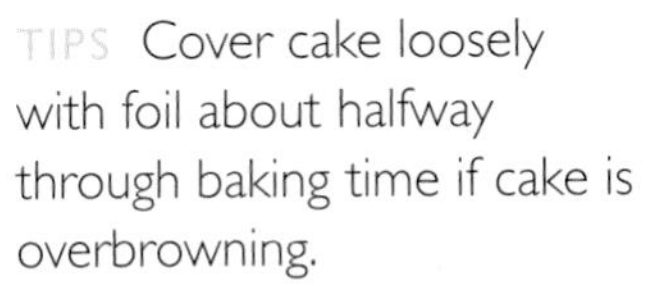

TIPS Cover cake loosely with foil about halfway through baking time if cake is overbrowning.
■ If you like the stronger flavours of treacle or molasses, substitute either one for the golden syrup.

STORAGE Frosted, this cake can be made 1 day ahead and kept in an airtight container; unfrosted, the cake will keep in an airtight container for up to 3 days.
■ Frosted or unfrosted, this cake can be frozen for up to 3 months.

TIPS Use two paper cases in each bun tray hole for added stability for butterfly cakes.

STORAGE Cakes are at their best made on day of serving. Once filled with cream, cakes should be refrigerated if made more than an hour ahead of time. ■ Unfilled cakes can be frozen for up to 1 month.

Spooning mixture into paper cases

Cutting small circles from tops of cakes

Filling cakes with jam and cream

butterfly cakes

Butterfly cakes are made by removing a small circle of cake from the top of each fairy cake, filling the cavity with your favourite jam and some cream, then topping the cream with the two halves of the circle to create 'wings'.

PREPARATION TIME 30 MINUTES BAKING TIME 20 MINUTES

125g BUTTER, SOFTENED
1 TEASPOON VANILLA ESSENCE
150g CASTER SUGAR
3 EGGS
225g SELF-RAISING FLOUR
60ml MILK
160g JAM
300ml WHIPPING CREAM

1 Line two deep 12-hole bun trays with paper cases.
2 Combine butter, essence, sugar, eggs, flour and milk in small bowl of electric mixer; beat on low speed until ingredients are just combined. Increase speed to medium, beat about 3 minutes, or until mixture is smooth and changed to a paler colour.
3 Drop slightly rounded tablespoons of mixture into paper cases. Bake in moderate oven about 20 minutes. Turn cakes onto wire racks, turn top-side up to cool.
4 Using sharp pointed vegetable knife, cut circle from top of each cake; cut circle in half to make two 'wings'. Fill cavities with jam and whipped cream. Place wings in position on top of cakes; top with strawberry pieces and dust with a little sifted icing sugar, if desired.

MAKES 24

STORAGE Un-iced cake can be made 2 days ahead and stored in an airtight container. ■ Un-iced cake can be frozen for up to 3 months.

devil's food cake

PREPARATION TIME 15 MINUTES BAKING TIME 45 MINUTES

180g BUTTER
385g CASTER SUGAR
3 EGGS
225g SELF-RAISING FLOUR
75g PLAIN FLOUR
½ TEASPOON BICARBONATE OF SODA
100g COCOA
3 TEASPOONS DRY INSTANT COFFEE
½ TEASPOON RED FOOD COLOURING
125ml WATER
125ml MILK

RICH CHOCOLATE FROSTING
60g DARK CHOCOLATE
60g UNSALTED BUTTER

1 Grease 2 deep 20cm (8in) round cake tins, line bases with baking parchment; grease paper.
2 Beat butter and sugar in small bowl with electric mixer until light and fluffy; add eggs one at a time, beating well after additions.
3 Transfer mixture to large bowl, fold in sifted flours, soda and cocoa with combined coffee, colouring, water and milk, in two batches.
4 Pour mixture into prepared tins; bake in moderate oven about 45 minutes. Turn cakes onto wire rack to cool. Join cold cakes with whipped or mock cream, top with rich chocolate frosting.

RICH CHOCOLATE FROSTING Combine chocolate and butter in heatproof bowl over pan of simmering water, stir until smooth. Remove from heat. Cool at room temperature until spreadable, stir occasionally while cooling.

SERVES 8

STORAGE Cake can be kept for up to 2 days stored in an airtight container.

Cake can be frozen for up to 3 months.

Believed to be of American origin, carrot cakes started to become very popular in the 1950s, and continue as favourites today. The cream cheese frosting adds a delicious richness.

carrot cake

PREPARATION TIME 15 MINUTES BAKING TIME 1 HOUR 30 MINUTES

250ml OIL
265g FIRMLY PACKED BROWN SUGAR
3 EGGS
3 MEDIUM CARROTS, COARSELY GRATED
120g CHOPPED WALNUTS OR PECANS
100g CHOPPED RAISINS
375g SELF-RAISING FLOUR
1/2 TEASPOON BICARBONATE OF SODA
2 TEASPOONS MIXED SPICE

CREAM CHEESE FROSTING
30g BUTTER
80g PACKAGED CREAM CHEESE, SOFTENED
1 TEASPOON GRATED LEMON RIND
1 TABLESPOON LEMON JUICE
240g ICING SUGAR

1 Grease 15cm x 25cm (6in x 10in) loaf tin, line base with baking parchment; grease paper.

2 Beat oil, sugar and eggs in small bowl with electric mixer until thick and creamy. Transfer mixture to large bowl; stir in carrot, nuts and raisins, then sifted dry ingredients.

3 Pour mixture into prepared pan; bake in moderate oven for 45 minutes.

4 Cover loosely with foil; bake about further 45 minutes. Stand a few minutes before turning onto wire rack to cool. Top cold cake with cream cheese frosting.

CREAM CHEESE FROSTING Beat butter, cheese, rind and juice in small bowl with electric mixer, beat until light and fluffy; gradually beat in sifted icing sugar.

SERVES 10

sacher torte

PREPARATION TIME 40 MINUTES
(PLUS STANDING TIME)
BAKING TIME 1 HOUR 10 MINUTES

100g DARK CHOCOLATE, CHOPPED COARSELY
250ml WATER
125g BUTTER, SOFTENED
250g FIRMLY PACKED BROWN SUGAR
3 EGGS
150g SELF-RAISING FLOUR
25g COCOA POWDER
60g GROUND ALMONDS
110g APRICOT JAM, WARMED, STRAINED
50g DARK CHOCOLATE, MELTED

GANACHE
200g DARK CHOCOLATE, CHOPPED COARSELY
160ml CREAM

1 Position oven shelves; preheat oven to moderately low. Grease deep 22cm (9in) round cake tin, line base with baking parchment.
2 Combine chopped chocolate and the water in small saucepan; using wooden spoon, stir over low heat until chocolate melts. Remove from heat.
3 Beat butter and sugar in small bowl with electric mixer until combined; beat in eggs, one at a time, only until combined. Mixture will curdle at this stage but will come together later.
4 Transfer mixture to large bowl; using wooden spoon, stir in sifted flour, cocoa, ground almonds and warm chocolate mixture. Mix well, pour into prepared tin.
5 Bake cake in moderately low oven about 1 hour and 10 minutes. Stand cake 10 minutes then turn onto wire rack; turn cake top-side up to cool.
6 Using serrated knife, split cold cake in half; sandwich layers with jam. Place cake on wire rack over tray; using metal spatula, spread a thin layer of ganache over cake.
7 Heat remaining ganache over saucepan of simmering water, stirring, until of pouring consistency; strain into medium jug. Using metal spatula and working quickly, pour ganache over cake, smoothing it all over top and side. Stand at room temperature until ganache sets.
8 Spoon melted chocolate into small paper piping bag; pipe SACHER on top of cake, allow to set at room temperature.

GANACHE Place chocolate and cream in small heatproof bowl; using wooden spoon, stir over small saucepan of simmering water until chocolate melts.

SERVES 12

TIPS Jam can be warmed in the microwave oven for about 10 seconds on HIGH (100%).
■ When melting chocolate in a bowl set over simmering water in a pan on top of the stove, it is important that the water never touches the bottom of the bowl. The bowl should be of such a size that it sits comfortably over a saucepan of complementary size.
■ Ganache sets at room temperature; if refrigerated, ganache will sweat.

STORAGE Iced cake can be kept up to 3 days in an airtight container in the refrigerator. Un-iced cake can be kept up to 1 week in an airtight container in the refrigerator.
■ Un-iced cake can be frozen for up to 3 months.

SACHER TORTE
This famous Viennese cake was originally made in 1832 by the grandfather of Eduard Sacher, founder of the Hotel Sacher, for the court of the Empire's Prince Metternich. The secret recipe was handed down to Eduard, who is responsible for popularising it on the hotel's menu... and on the menu of restaurants and cafes throughout the world.

dundee cake

180g BUTTER, SOFTENED
165g CASTER SUGAR
5 EGGS, LIGHTLY BEATEN
225g PLAIN FLOUR
75g SELF-RAISING FLOUR
½ TEASPOON MIXED SPICE
85ml MILK
250g RAISINS, CHOPPED
250g CURRANTS
250g SULTANAS
2 TABLESPOONS MIXED PEEL
70g GLACÉ CHERRIES, CHOPPED
2 TABLESPOONS BLANCHED ALMONDS
RED GLACÉ CHERRIES, EXTRA
BLANCHED ALMONDS, EXTRA
1 TABLESPOON BRANDY

PREPARATION TIME 20 MINUTES BAKING TIME 3 HOURS

1 Line deep 20cm (8in) round cake tin with 3 layers of baking parchment, bringing paper 5cm (2in) above edge of tin.
2 Beat butter, sugar, eggs, sifted dry ingredients and milk in large bowl with electric mixer on medium speed about 3 minutes or until mixture changes colour slightly. Stir in fruit and nuts, mix well.
3 Spread mixture into prepared pan, decorate top with extra cherries and nuts. Bake in low oven about 3 hours. Brush hot cake with brandy; cover with foil, cool in tin.

SERVES 12

STORAGE Cake can be kept for up to a week stored in an airtight container.

■ Cake can be frozen for up to 3 months.

boiled fruit cake

PREPARATION TIME 25 MINUTES BAKING TIME 2 HOURS

500g MIXED DRIED FRUIT, CHOPPED
125ml WATER
200g BROWN SUGAR, FIRMLY PACKED
125g BUTTER
1 TEASPOON MIXED SPICE
½ TEASPOON BICARBONATE OF SODA
125ml SWEET SHERRY
1 EGG, LIGHTLY BEATEN
150g PLAIN FLOUR
150g SELF-RAISING FLOUR
BLANCHED ALMONDS
2 TABLESPOONS SWEET SHERRY, EXTRA

1 Combine fruit, water, sugar, butter, spice and soda in large pan; stir over heat, without boiling, until sugar is dissolved and butter melted. Bring to boil; cover, simmer 5 minutes. Remove from heat, stir in sherry; cover, cool.

2 Grease deep 20cm (8in) round cake tin; line base and side with 2 thicknesses of baking parchment, bringing paper 5cm (2in) above edge of tin.

3 Stir egg and sifted flours into fruit mixture.

4 Spread mixture into prepared tin, decorate top with almonds. Bake in moderately slow oven about 2 hours. Brush top of hot cake with extra sherry. Cover cake with foil, cool in pan.

SERVES 12

TIPS Boiled fruit cake is quicker and less expensive to make than the traditional baked fruit cake.
The boiled fruit mixture is best left to cool slowly overnight.

STORAGE Cake can be kept for up to 2 weeks stored in an airtight container.
Cake can be frozen for up to 3 months.

STORAGE Poppy seed loaf can be made a day ahead and stored in an airtight container.; caraway seed loaf can be made 2 days ahead and stored in an airtight container. ■ Both cakes can be frozen for up to 3 months.

poppy seed loaf

PREPARATION TIME 15 MINUTES (PLUS STANDING TIME)
BAKING TIME 1 HOUR

50g POPPY SEEDS
185ml MILK
180g BUTTER, SOFTENED
2 TEASPOONS VANILLA ESSENCE
220g CASTER SUGAR
3 EGGS, LIGHTLY BEATEN
300g SELF-RAISING FLOUR

1 Grease 14cm x 21cm (5½in x 8in) loaf tin, line base with baking parchment; grease paper.
2 Combine poppy seeds and milk in medium bowl; cover, stand 1 hour.
3 Add butter, essence, sugar, eggs and sifted flour to poppy seed mixture; beat mixture on low speed with electric mixer until combined. Beat on medium speed about 3 minutes or until mixture is slightly changed in colour.
4 Pour mixture into prepared tin; bake in moderate oven about 1 hour. Stand in tin 5 minutes before turning onto wire rack to cool.

SERVES 12

HOW TO TEST IF A CAKE IS COOKED

Test cake just before the cooking time has expired. Touch top of cake with fingers; if it is firm, test using skewer in the thickest part of the cake, but not through a crack. If the skewer comes out free from any cake mixture, remove cake from oven. If cake mixture does appear on the skewer, test cake again after further 5 minutes of cooking. Shake pan gently to make sure the cake is free from pan. Turn cake onto wire rack. Then, so that the rack does not mark the top of the cake, invert cake onto wire rack to finish cooling.

caraway seed loaf

PREPARATION TIME 15 MINUTES BAKING TIME 50 MINUTES

180g BUTTER
145g CASTER SUGAR
3 EGGS
1 TABLESPOON CARAWAY SEEDS
225g SELF-RAISING FLOUR
62ml MILK

1 Grease 14cm x 21cm (5½in x 8in) loaf tin.
2 Beat butter and sugar in small bowl with electric mixer until light and fluffy; beat in eggs, 1 at a time, until combined.
3 Transfer mixture to large bowl; stir in seeds, sifted flour and milk.
4 Spread mixture into prepared tin; bake in moderate oven about 1 hour.

SERVES 12

poppy seed loaf (above)
caraway seed loaf (below)

apple streusel cake

This cake, completely finished after baking since it has its own topping, is simply delicious. We used Granny Smith apples in our version.

PREPARATION TIME 20 MINUTES (PLUS FREEZING TIME)
BAKING TIME 50 MINUTES

3 MEDIUM APPLES (450g)
1 TABLESPOON CASTER SUGAR
60ml WATER
185g BUTTER, SOFTENED
165g CASTER SUGAR, EXTRA
2 EGGS
335g SELF-RAISING FLOUR
180ml MILK

CINNAMON STREUSEL TOPPING
110g PLAIN FLOUR
3 TEASPOONS GROUND CINNAMON
60g BUTTER, CHOPPED
75g FIRMLY PACKED BROWN SUGAR
2 TEASPOONS WATER, APPROXIMATELY

1 Position oven shelves; preheat oven to moderate. Grease deep 23cm (9in) square cake tin; line base with baking archment.
2 Peel, core and quarter apples; slice thinly. Combine apple, sugar and the water in medium saucepan; bring to a boil. Reduce heat; simmer, covered, about 10 minutes or until apple is tender, drain well.
3 Meanwhile, beat butter and extra sugar in small bowl with electric mixer until light and fluffy. Add eggs, one at a time, beating well between additions. Transfer mixture to large bowl; using wooden spoon, stir in flour and milk, in two batches.
4 Spread two-thirds of the mixture evenly over base of prepared tin, top evenly with apple, then spread with remaining mixture. Sprinkle evenly with cinnamon streusel topping.
5 Bake cake in moderate oven about 50 minutes. Stand cake 5 minutes then turn onto wire rack; turn cake top-side up to cool.

CINNAMON STREUSEL TOPPING Combine flour and cinnamon in small bowl; rub in butter with fingertips, add sugar. Using one hand, mix in enough of the water to make mixture come together in a ball, cover with cling film; freeze 30 minutes. Coarsely grate topping mixture before sprinkling on unbaked cake.

SERVES 12

Layering apple over cake mixture

Coarsely grating streusel topping mixture

Sprinkling streusel topping over cake mixture

TIPS Canned pie apple can be used instead of fresh apples. If using canned apple, omit apples, sugar and water from ingredient list.

Any other stewed or canned fruit can be substituted for apple but ensure the fruit is as dry as possible; excess moisture will make the cake doughy. Fruit canned in water or syrup should be drained then placed on kitchen paper for at least 10 minutes.

Cake can also be baked in a 20cm x 30cm (8in x 12in) baking tin, its base lined with baking parchment. Bake cake in moderate oven about 50 minutes.

STORAGE Apple streusel cake can be kept for up to 2 days stored in an airtight container at room temperature, or in the refrigerator for up to 3 days.

STORAGE Cake can be made a day ahead and stored in an airtight container.
■ Cake can be frozen for up to 3 months.

madeira cake

PREPARATION TIME 15 MINUTES
BAKING TIME 1 HOUR

180g BUTTER, SOFTENED
2 TEASPOONS GRATED LEMON RIND
145g CASTER SUGAR
3 EGGS
112g PLAIN FLOUR
112g SELF-RAISING FLOUR
55g MIXED PEEL
20g SLIVERED ALMONDS

1 Grease deep 20cm (8in) round cake tin, line base with baking parchment; grease paper.
2 Beat butter, rind and sugar in small bowl with electric mixer until light and fluffy; beat in eggs, 1 at a time, until combined.
3 Transfer mixture to large bowl, stir in sifted flours.
4 Spread mixture into prepared tin; bake in moderately low oven 20 minutes. Sprinkle peel and nuts evenly over cake. Bake about further 40 minutes. Stand cake 5 minutes before turning onto wire rack to cool.

SERVES 12

This cake does not actually contain madeira. It is a plain cake, always topped with peel, and was served with a glass of madeira in Victorian England.

strawberry shortcake

PREPARATION TIME 20 MINUTES BAKING TIME 20 MINUTES

250g BUTTER
1 TEASPOON GRATED LEMON RIND
1 TABLESPOON LEMON JUICE
110g CASTER SUGAR
50g RICE FLOUR OR GROUND RICE
150g SELF-RAISING FLOUR
200g PLAIN FLOUR
250g PUNNET STRAWBERRIES, HALVED
160g STRAWBERRY JAM

1 Lightly grease 26cm (10in) recessed flan tin.
2 Have butter at room temperature. Beat butter, rind, juice and sugar in small bowl with electric mixer until creamy. Stir in sifted flours in 2 batches. Press ingredients together gently, knead lightly until smooth.
3 Press dough evenly into prepared tin. Bake in moderate oven about 20 minutes or until lightly browned; cool in tin.
4 Turn shortcake onto serving plate, decorate with berries. Warm jam in small pan; strain, brush evenly over strawberries.

SERVES 12

SHORTCAKE
Although associated with America, the shortcake in fact originated in England and Europe. In England it was known as shortbread, until that name came to be used exclusively for the New Year Scottish shortbreads.
■ As an alternative to rice flour, use fine semolina.

STORAGE Shortcake can be made a week ahead; store covered, in refrigerator. Assemble cake just before serving.
■ Shortcake can be frozen for up to 3 months.

mississippi mud cake

250g BUTTER, CHOPPED COARSELY
150g DARK CHOCOLATE, CHOPPED COARSELY
440g CASTER SUGAR
250ml HOT WATER
80ml COFFEE LIQUEUR
1 TABLESPOON INSTANT COFFEE POWDER
225g PLAIN FLOUR
35g SELF-RAISING FLOUR
25g COCOA POWDER
2 EGGS, BEATEN LIGHTLY

PREPARATION TIME 25 MINUTES BAKING TIME 1 HOUR 30 MINUTES

1 Position oven shelves; preheat oven to moderately low. Grease deep 20cm (8in) round cake tin; line base and side with baking parchment.
2 Combine butter, chocolate, sugar, the water, liqueur and coffee powder in medium saucepan. Using wooden spoon, stir over low heat until chocolate melts.
3 Transfer mixture to large bowl; cool 15 minutes. Whisk in combined sifted flours and cocoa, then eggs. Pour mixture into prepared tin.
4 Bake cake in moderately slow oven about 1½ hours. Stand cake 30 minutes then turn onto wire rack, turn cake top-side up to cool.

SERVES 16

This popular cake is a delectable alternative to fruit cake for weddings and other occasions. It is also wonderful after dinner with coffee, served warm or at room temperature with whipped cream and berries.

Coarsely chopping chocolate

Adding chocolate to saucepan

TIPS Any coffee or chocolate-flavoured liqueur (Tia Maria, Kahlua or Crème de Cacao) can be used in this recipe.
■ Cover cake loosely with foil about halfway through the baking time if it starts to overbrown.
■ The melted chocolate mixture can be made in a large microwave-safe bowl on HIGH (100%) in the microwave oven for about 3 minutes, pausing to stir four times during cooking time.

STORAGE Cake can be kept for up to 1 week stored in an airtight container in the refrigerator.
■ Cake can be frozen for up to 3 months.

STORAGE Scones best made just before serving.
■ Scones can be frozen for up to 3 months.

buttermilk scones

PREPARATION TIME 20 MINUTES BAKING TIME 15 MINUTES

450g SELF-RAISING FLOUR
1/4 TEASPOON SALT
1 TEASPOON ICING SUGAR
60g BUTTER
430ml BUTTERMILK, APPROXIMATELY

1 Grease 23cm (9in) square shallow baking tin.
2 Sift dry ingredients into large bowl, rub in butter. Stir in enough buttermilk to mix to a soft, sticky dough.
3 Turn dough onto floured surface, knead until smooth. Press dough out to 2cm (¾in) thickness, cut to 5.5cm (2¼in) rounds.
4 Place rounds in prepared tin; bake in very hot oven about 15 minutes.

MAKES 16

SCONES served hot from the oven with butter or jam and cream are delightful for morning or afternoon tea. Often, cooks are judged by the scones they can make. There is no mystery about making light, fluffy scones; you must make a soft, sticky dough and the dough should be kneaded quickly and lightly. The rest is up to the oven; it should be very hot to make the scones rise quickly.

eccles cakes

It is thought the Crusaders introduced these to England when they returned from the Holy Land in the 13th century.

PREPARATION TIME 20 MINUTES BAKING TIME 15 MINUTES

3 SHEETS READY-ROLLED PUFF PASTRY
1 EGG YOLK, LIGHTLY BEATEN
CASTER SUGAR

FILLING
30g BUTTER
125g CURRANTS
42g CHOPPED MIXED PEEL
2 TABLESPOONS CASTER SUGAR
½ TEASPOON GROUND NUTMEG
½ TEASPOON MIXED SPICE

1 Cut pastry into 11cm (4¼in) rounds. Place a level tablespoon of filling in centre of each round. Pinch edges together to enclose filling. Turn smooth-side up onto floured surface, flatten gently with rolling pin so that currants just show through pastry.
2 Shape into oval cakes, place on greased oven trays. Brush cakes with egg yolk, sprinkle lightly with sugar, cut 3 small slits in top of each cake.
3 Bake cakes in moderately hot oven about 15 minutes or until browned.

FILLING Combine butter, fruit, sugar and spices in pan, stir over low heat until butter is melted; cool.

MAKES 12

STORAGE Eccles cakes can be kept for up to 2 days stored in an airtight container. ■ Eccles cakes can be frozen for up to 3 months.

Simmering water, sugar, butter, cocoa and soda

Pouring mixture into prepared tin

TIPS Choose a perfectly level-bottomed baking tin; one made from cast aluminium is the best choice, but almost any type will work.

If the cake appears to be cooking too quickly in the corners of the tin, reduce oven temperature to moderately low; this will increase cooking time by up to 15 minutes.

STORAGE Cake will keep for up to 2 days in an airtight container at room temperature, or in the refrigerator for up to 4 days.

Frosted or unfrosted, this cake can be frozen for up to 1 month.

family chocolate cake

PREPARATION TIME 20 MINUTES BAKING TIME 50 MINUTES

One saucepan plus one large, heavy baking tin are practically all the equipment needed to put together this easy, yummy chocolate cake.

500ml WATER
660g CASTER SUGAR
250g BUTTER, CHOPPED
35g COCOA POWDER
1 TEASPOON BICARBONATE OF SODA
450g SELF-RAISING FLOUR
4 EGGS, BEATEN LIGHTLY

FUDGE FROSTING
90g BUTTER
80ml WATER
110g CASTER SUGAR
240g ICING SUGAR
35g COCOA POWDER

1 Preheat oven to moderate. Grease deep 26.5cm x 33cm (10½in x 13in) (3.5-litre) baking tin; line base with baking parchment.
2 Combine water, sugar, butter and combined sifted cocoa and soda in medium saucepan; stir over heat, without boiling, until sugar dissolves. Bring to a boil then reduce heat; simmer, uncovered, 5 minutes. Transfer mixture to large bowl; cool to room temperature.
3 Add flour and eggs to bowl; beat with electric mixer until mixture is smooth and changed to a paler colour. Pour mixture into prepared tin.
4 Bake cake in moderate oven about 50 minutes. Stand cake 10 minutes then turn onto wire rack; turn cake top-side up to cool.
5 Spread cold cake with fudge frosting.

FUDGE FROSTING Combine butter, the water and caster sugar in small saucepan; stir over heat, without boiling, until sugar dissolves. Sift icing sugar and cocoa into small bowl then gradually stir in hot butter mixture. Cover; refrigerate about 20 minutes or until frosting thickens. Beat with wooden spoon until spreadable.

SERVES 20

rock cakes

300g SELF-RAISING FLOUR
¼ TEASPOON GROUND CINNAMON
90g BUTTER
75g CASTER SUGAR
160g SULTANAS
2 TABLESPOONS MIXED PEEL
1 EGG, LIGHTLY BEATEN
125ml MILK, APPROXIMATELY
1 TABLESPOON CASTER SUGAR, EXTRA

STORAGE Cakes can be kept for up to 3 days stored in an airtight container.
■ Rock cakes can be frozen for up to 3 months.

PREPARATION TIME 20 MINUTES BAKING TIME 15 MINUTES

1 Sift flour and cinnamon into large bowl, rub in butter, stir in sugar and fruit. Stir in egg, then enough milk to give a moist but firm consistency.
2 Place 2-level-tablespoon portions of mixture onto lightly greased oven trays about 5cm (2in) apart. Sprinkle cakes with a little extra sugar.
3 Bake in moderately hot oven about 15 minutes or until browned. Loosen cakes; cool on trays.

MAKES ABOUT 18

TIP Apricot nectar is the juice of apricots. If you can't find the juice in the supermarket, buy tinned apricots and blend them to a pulp.

STORAGE Cake can be kept for up to 3 days stored in an airtight container.

150g CHOPPED DRIED APRICOTS
250ml APRICOT NECTAR
125g BUTTER, SOFTENED
150g RAW SUGAR
2 EGGS, SEPARATED
120g DESICCATED COCONUT
225g SELF-RAISING FLOUR
95g DARK CHOCOLATE CHIPS

apricot chocolate chip cake

PREPARATION TIME 30 MINUTES (PLUS STANDING TIME)
BAKING TIME 1 HOUR 15 MINUTES

1 Preheat oven to moderate (180°C/160°C fan-assisted). Grease deep 20cm (8in) round cake tin; line base with baking parchment.
2 Combine apricots and nectar in medium bowl; stand 1 hour.
3 Beat butter and sugar in small bowl with electric mixer until light and fluffy. Add egg yolks, beat until combined.
4 Transfer mixture to large bowl, stir in coconut then half the sifted flour and half the apricot mixture. Stir in remaining flour, remaining apricot mixture then chocolate chips
5 Beat egg whites in small bowl with electric mixer until soft peaks form; fold into apricot mixture.
6 Spread mixture into tin; bake about 1¼ hours. Stand cake for 5 minutes before turning onto wire rack to cool.
7 Serve cake dusted with sifted icing sugar, if desired.

SERVES 8

biscuits, cookies & slices

BISCUIT BAKING TIPS

- If butter has to be creamed, it should be at room temperature.
- Don't over-stir a biscuit mixture.
- Use flat baking trays or those with tiny sides. Or turn a flat baking tin upside down and use the base for baking.
- Grease trays lightly.
- Be careful not to over-cook biscuits; they will become crisp when they're cold. They still should feel a little soft when cooked. Usually, the biscuits around the outside edge of the tray will be cooked first.
- Don't be afraid to open the oven during cooking, and move the trays. This helps biscuits to brown evenly. Also, turn the trays; some ovens tend to cook too quickly towards the back of the oven.

coffee snaps

PREPARATION TIME 15 MINUTES BAKING TIME 10 MINUTES PER TRAY

125g BUTTER, SOFTENED
275g FIRMLY PACKED BROWN SUGAR
3 TEASPOONS GROUND COFFEE
½ TEASPOON VANILLA EXTRACT
1 EGG
110g PLAIN FLOUR
110g SELF-RAISING FLOUR
70 COFFEE BEANS

1 Preheat oven to moderate (180°C/160°C fan-assisted).
2 Beat butter, sugar, coffee and extract in small bowl with electric mixer until light and fluffy. Add egg; beat until just combined. Stir in sifted flours.
3 Roll rounded teaspoons of mixture into balls. Place 3cm (1in) apart on greased baking trays. Top each with a coffee bean. Bake in moderate oven about 10 minutes. Transfer to wire racks to cool.

MAKES 70

STORAGE Coffee snaps can be kept for up to a week stored in an airtight container.

STORAGE Cookies can be kept for up to 4 days stored in an airtight container.
■ Cookies are suitable for freezing.

chocolate chip cookies

PREPARATION TIME 10 MINUTES BAKING TIME 12 MINUTES

90g BUTTER
1 TEASPOON VANILLA ESSENCE
75g CASTER SUGAR
65g BROWN SUGAR
1 EGG
75g SELF-RAISING FLOUR
112g PLAIN FLOUR
142g CHOCOLATE CHIPS
50g CHOPPED PECANS OR WALNUTS
1 TABLESPOON MILK

1 Beat butter, essence and sugars in small bowl with electric mixer until light and fluffy, beat in egg. Stir in flours, chocolate chips, nuts and milk.
2 Drop heaped tablespoons of mixture onto lightly greased baking trays, about 3cm (1in) apart.
3 Bake in moderate oven about 12 minutes or until firm and lightly browned. Stand on trays 5 minutes then lift onto wire racks to cool.

MAKES ABOUT 18

CHOCOLATE CHIP COOKIES One story suggests that these were created by a housewife in Massachusetts, in the United States, in 1929. They are also known as Toll House Cookies.

CHOCOLATE CHIPS are available in milk, white and dark chocolate. Made of cocoa liquor, cocoa butter, sugar and an emulsifier, they hold their shape in baking and are ideal for decorating cakes.

melting moments

Melting moments, or yo-yos, have a long history. There is even a recipe for them in Mrs Beeton's Cookery and Household Management.

125g BUTTER
1 TEASPOON VANILLA ESSENCE
2 TABLESPOONS ICING SUGAR
112g PLAIN FLOUR
37g CORNFLOUR

FILLING
30g BUTTER
½ TEASPOON VANILLA ESSENCE
80g ICING SUGAR
1 TEASPOON MILK, APPROXIMATELY

PREPARATION TIME 15 MINUTES BAKING TIME 10 MINUTES

1 Beat butter, essence and sifted icing sugar in small bowl with electric mixer until light and fluffy. Stir in sifted flours.
2 Spoon mixture into piping bag fitted with a 1cm (½in) fluted tube. Pipe 3cm (1¼in) rosettes about 3cm (1in) apart onto lightly greased baking trays.
3 Bake in moderate oven about 10 minutes or until lightly browned; cool on trays. Join cold biscuits with filling.

FILLING Beat butter, essence and sifted icing sugar in small bowl until light and fluffy; beat in enough milk to make mixture spreadable.

MAKES ABOUT 20

STORAGE Biscuits can be kept for up to 2 days stored in an airtight container.
■ Unfilled biscuits suitable for freezing.

STORAGE Shortbread drops can be kept for up to a week stored in an airtight container.

almond shortbread drops

PREPARATION TIME 15 MINUTES BAKING TIME 20 MINUTES

60g BUTTER, CHOPPED
75g PLAIN FLOUR
1 TABLESPOON RICE FLOUR
2 TABLESPOONS ICING SUGAR
12 BLANCHED ALMONDS

1 Preheat oven to moderately low (160°C/140°C fan-assisted).
2 Process butter, flours and icing sugar until mixture forms a ball. Knead gently on floured surface until smooth.
3 Roll 2 teaspoons of mixture into balls; place on greased baking tray about 3cm (1in) apart. Top each ball with an almond.
4 Bake in moderately low oven about 20 minutes or until browned lightly. Cool on tray.

MAKES 12

STORAGE Slices can be kept for up to a week stored in an airtight container. ■ Slice suitable for freezing.

garibaldi slices

These biscuits were unkindly called 'squashed flies' by children, due to the appearance of the filling.

PREPARATION TIME 20 MINUTES (PLUS REFRIGERATION TIME)
BAKING TIME 40 MINUTES

85g CURRANTS
100g RAISINS
240g SULTANAS
450g PLAIN FLOUR
250g BUTTER, CHOPPED
75g CASTER SUGAR
2 EGG YOLKS
2 TABLESPOONS WATER, APPROXIMATELY
CASTER SUGAR, EXTRA

1 Grease 26cm x 32cm (10in x 12in) Swiss roll tin. Blend or process dried fruit until chopped.
2 Sift flour into bowl, rub in butter, stir in sugar. Add yolks and enough water to mix to a soft dough. Turn dough onto floured surface, knead lightly until smooth; cover, refrigerate 30 minutes.
3 Divide dough in half; roll 1 portion between sheets of baking parchment until large enough to fit base of prepared tin. Lift pastry into tin. Spread with fruit. Roll remaining pastry large enough to cover fruit; place over fruit. Press all over with hand to join slice; trim edges.
4 Score into rectangles through top layer of pastry. Brush with a little water, sprinkle with a little extra sugar; prick with fork.
5 Bake in moderately hot oven 10 minutes. Reduce heat to moderate; bake about further 30 minutes or until browned. Cut slices while hot; cool in tin.

MAKES AROUND 36

STORAGE Biscuits can be kept for up to a week stored in an airtight container.
■ Gingernuts suitable for freezing.

gingernuts

Ginger has long been used as a flavouring for biscuits. These deliciously crisp gingernuts are also known as ginger snaps.

PREPARATION TIME 10 MINUTES
BAKING TIME 12 MINUTES

90g BUTTER
65g BROWN SUGAR
115g GOLDEN SYRUP
200g PLAIN FLOUR
3/4 TEASPOON BICARBONATE OF SODA
1 TEASPOON GROUND CINNAMON
1 TABLESPOON GROUND GINGER
1/4 TEASPOON GROUND CLOVES

1 Combine butter, sugar and golden syrup in pan; stir over heat until butter is melted. Remove from heat, stir in sifted dry ingredients; stand until mixture feels warm to the touch.
2 Roll 2-level-teaspoon portions of mixture into balls, place about 3cm (1in) apart on greased baking trays; flatten slightly.
3 Bake in moderate oven about 12 minutes or until browned. Loosen biscuits; cool on baking trays.

MAKES ABOUT 35

STORAGE Brownies can be kept for up to 3 days stored in an airtight container.

triple choc brownies

PREPARATION TIME 20 MINUTES BAKING TIME 35 MINUTES

125g BUTTER, CHOPPED
200g DARK EATING CHOCOLATE, CHOPPED COARSELY
110g CASTER SUGAR
2 EGGS, BEATEN LIGHTLY
185g PLAIN FLOUR
150g WHITE EATING CHOCOLATE, CHOPPED COARSELY
100g MILK EATING CHOCOLATE, CHOPPED COARSELY

1 Preheat oven to moderate (180°C/160°C fan-assisted). Grease deep 19cm (7½in) square cake tin; line base and sides with baking parchment.
2 Combine butter and dark chocolate in medium saucepan; stir over low heat until melted. Cool 10 minutes.
3 Stir in sugar and egg, then flour; stir in white and milk chocolates. Spread mixture into tin.
4 Bake about 35 minutes or until mixture is firm to touch. Cool in pan. If desired, sprinkle with sifted icing sugar before cutting.

SERVES 12

STORAGE Shortbread can be kept for up to a month stored in an airtight container.
■ Shortbread suitable for freezing.

SHORTBREAD
Originally a Hogmanay specialty of Scotland, where it originated up to 400 years ago, shortbread has become very popular in many parts of the globe and is now eaten all year.
■ As an alternative to rice flour, use fine semolina.
■ Try adding 50g chopped glace ginger or 1tablespoon finely grated orange rind to spice up the flavour of the shortbread.

shortbread

PREPARATION TIME 20 MINUTES BAKING TIME 12 MINUTES

250g BUTTER
75g CASTER SUGAR
300g PLAIN FLOUR
90g RICE FLOUR OR GROUND RICE

1 Have butter at room temperature. Beat butter and sugar in small bowl with electric mixer until combined. Add large spoonfuls of sifted flours to butter mixture, beating after each addition.
2 Press ingredients together gently, knead on floured surface until smooth.
3 Divide dough into 2 portions; shape portions into 18cm (7in) rounds. Place rounds on greased baking trays; mark into wedges, prick with fork. Pinch a decorative edge with floured fingers.
4 Bake in low oven about 30 minutes. Stand 10 minutes before transferring to wire rack to cool. Cut when cold.

MAKES 2 SHORTBREAD ROUNDS

TIP The caramel filling must be stirred constantly during cooking for perfect results.

STORAGE Slices can be kept for up to 3 days stored in an airtight container.

caramel chocolate slices

PREPARATION TIME 10 MINUTES BAKING TIME 25 MINUTES

150g SELF-RAISING FLOUR
90g COCONUT
200g BROWN SUGAR, FIRMLY PACKED
125g BUTTER, MELTED

FILLING
400g CAN SWEETENED CONDENSED MILK
30g BUTTER
2 TABLESPOONS GOLDEN SYRUP

TOPPING
125g DARK CHOCOLATE, CHOPPED
30g BUTTER

1 Lightly grease 20cm x 30cm (8in x 12in) shallow baking tin.
2 Combine sifted flour, coconut and sugar in bowl; add butter, stir until combined.
3 Press mixture over base of prepared tin. Bake in moderate oven 15 minutes.
4 Pour hot filling over hot base, return to oven 10 minutes; cool.
5 Spread warm topping over filling, stand at room temperature until set.

FILLING Combine milk, butter and golden syrup in pan; stir over low heat, without boiling, about 15 minutes or until mixture is golden brown.

TOPPING Combine chocolate and butter in pan; stir over low heat until smooth.

MAKES AROUND 24

rich mocha fudge

PREPARATION TIME 20 MINUTES COOKING TIME 15 MINUTES (PLUS COOLING AND REFRIGERATION TIME)

220g CASTER SUGAR
160g SOURED CREAM
2 TABLESPOONS GLUCOSE SYRUP
250g DARK COOKING CHOCOLATE, FINELY CHOPPED
100g PACKET WHITE MARSHMALLOWS, ROUGHLY CHOPPED
2 TABLESPOONS COFFEE-FLAVOURED LIQUEUR
2 TABLESPOONS DRY INSTANT COFFEE
2 TEASPOONS BOILING WATER
30 CHOCOLATE-COATED COFFEE BEANS

1 Grease 8cm x 25cm (4in x 10in) shallow cake tin; line base and two long sides with baking parchment.
2 Combine sugar, soured cream and glucose in small saucepan; stir over low heat, without boiling, until sugar dissolves. Using pastry brush dipped in hot water, brush down side of pan to dissolve any sugar crystals; bring to a boil. Boil, uncovered, without stirring, about 10 minutes or until syrup reaches 155°C when measured on a sugar thermometer.
3 Remove from heat; add chocolate and marshmallow, stir until melted. Stir in combined liqueur, coffee and the boiling water.
4 Spread mixture into prepared tin; cool. Cover; refrigerate until firm.
5 Cut into 30 small squares; top each with a chocolate-coated coffee bean.

MAKES 30 PIECES

- A sugar thermometer is a worthwhile investment if you intend using it fairly often. It takes the guesswork out of making sweets.
- Place the thermometer in a pan of cold water and bring to a boil. Check it registers accurately on boiling point (100°C or 212°F); make allowances for any inaccuracies when gauging the syrup.
- Never plunge it into boiling syrup without this preparation or it will probably break.
- When syrup reaches required temperature, remove thermometer; return to pan of boiling water. Remove from heat; cool to room temperature in the water.

TIP You can use a hazelnut-flavoured liqueur instead of the coffee-flavoured liqueur and top each piece with a halved hazelnut, if preferred.

STORAGE The fudge can be made up to four weeks ahead. Store, covered, in the refrigerator.

TIP Grand Marnier can be substituted for the Cointreau.

STORAGE This recipe can be made a week ahead; roll truffles in cocoa 3 hours before serving.

rich chocolate truffles

PREPARATION TIME 20 MINUTES (PLUS STANDING TIME)
COOKING TIME 5 MINUTES (PLUS COOLING TIME)

200g DARK CHOCOLATE, CHOPPED COARSELY
2 TABLESPOONS CREAM
1 TABLESPOON COINTREAU
35g COCOA POWDER

1 Combine chocolate and cream in medium heatproof bowl over medium saucepan of barely simmering water; stir until smooth. Remove from heat; cool. Stir in liqueur. Cover; stand at room temperature 3 hours or until firm.
2 Roll 2 level teaspoons of the mixture into balls. Place sifted cocoa in medium bowl. Toss balls to coat in cocoa; shake away excess cocoa. Refrigerate truffles in an airtight container.

MAKES 20

rum balls

PREPARATION TIME 10 MINUTES CHILLING TIME 2 HOURS

400g FINE CAKE CRUMBS
25g COCOA
80g APRICOT JAM, WARMED
2 TABLESPOONS DARK RUM
2 TABLESPOONS WATER
185g CHOCOLATE SPRINKLES

1 Combine crumbs and sifted cocoa in bowl; stir in combined strained jam, rum and water.
2 Roll 2 level teaspoons of mixture into balls. Roll balls in chocolate sprinkles. Refrigerate 2 hours before serving.

MAKES ABOUT 45

STORAGE Rum balls can be kept for up to a week stored, covered, in the refrigerator.

STORAGE Truffles can be kept for up to 2 weeks stored in an airtight container in the refrigerator.

white chocolate snowball truffles

PREPARATION TIME 40 MINUTES COOKING TIME 5 MINUTES (PLUS REFRIGERATION TIME)

60ml CREAM
30g BUTTER
250g WHITE EATING CHOCOLATE, CHOPPED FINELY
70g SLIVERED ALMONDS, TOASTED
1 TABLESPOON ALMOND LIQUEUR
250g WHITE EATING CHOCOLATE, MELTED, EXTRA
90g DESICCATED COCONUT

1 Heat cream and butter in small saucepan; bring to a boil. Place chopped chocolate in medium heatproof bowl; add cream mixture, stir until smooth.
2 Stir in the almonds and liqueur. Cover and refrigerate, stirring occasionally, for about 30 minutes or until mixture begins to thicken. Roll rounded teaspoons of the mixture into balls; place in a single layer on cling film-lined tray. Refrigerate until firm.
3 Dip truffles into melted chocolate; gently shake off excess chocolate. Roll wet truffles in coconut; return to tray. Refrigerate until firm.

MAKES 30

STORAGE Florentines can be kept for up to 3 days stored in an airtight container.

mini florentines

PREPARATION TIME 45 MINUTES BAKING TIME 30 MINUTES

30g BUTTER
2 TABLESPOONS BROWN SUGAR
1 TEASPOON GOLDEN SYRUP
¼ TEASPOON GROUND GINGER
1 TABLESPOON PLAIN FLOUR
2 TEASPOONS MIXED PEEL
1 TABLESPOON FINELY CHOPPED RED GLACÉ CHERRIES
20g FLAKED ALMONDS, CHOPPED COARSELY
75g DARK CHOCOLATE

1 Preheat oven to moderate. Combine butter, sugar and syrup in small saucepan; stir over heat, without boiling, until sugar dissolves. Remove from heat.
2 Stir in ginger and flour, then mixed peel, cherries and nuts. Drop level ½ teaspoons of mixture onto greased baking trays, leaving about 6cm (2½in) between each to allow mixture to spread. Cook in batches of six at a time.
3 Bake in moderate oven about 5 minutes or until golden brown; gently push florentines into shape with a small cutter or palette knife while still hot. Stand florentines 1 minute before transferring to wire rack to cool.
4 Melt chocolate; spread chocolate over flat side of florentines; run a fork through chocolate, before it sets, to make a wavy pattern. Stand florentines, chocolate-side up, on wire rack until set.

MAKES 36

coconut macaroons

Although almonds are the key ingredient in traditional macaroons, coconut quickly became an equally popular adaptation.

PREPARATION TIME 15 MINUTES COOKING TIME 40 MINUTES

2 EGG WHITES
110g CASTER SUGAR
1 TEASPOON VANILLA ESSENCE
2 TABLESPOONS PLAIN FLOUR
140g COCONUT
6 GLACÉ CHERRIES, QUARTERED

1 Beat egg whites in small bowl with electric mixer until soft peaks form. Gradually add sugar, beating until dissolved after additions. Stir in essence, sifted flour and coconut in 2 batches.

2 Line baking trays with baking parchment. Drop level tablespoons of mixture onto trays about 5cm (2in) apart. Place a cherry quarter on top of each macaroon.

3 Bake in low oven about 40 minutes or until lightly browned; cool on trays.

MAKES ABOUT 25

STORAGE Macaroons can be kept for up to a week stored in an airtight container.

■ Macaroons are suitable for freezing.

pies & tarts

apple pie

PASTRY TIPS

■ Resting: wrap pastry in plastic and refrigerate up to 30 minutes before and after rolling. This 'rests' the pastry by relaxing the gluten (protein) in the flour and helps to prevent shrinkage during baking.
■ Rolling: roll pastry evenly on lightly floured surface, using only enough flour to prevent dough sticking; a cold surface is best. Roll from centre, outwards, each time rolling pastry towards you and away from you using short light strokes. Reduce pressure towards edges; do not roll over the edges.
■ Storing and freezing: pastry can be kept in a refrigerator, wrapped securely in plastic, 2 days, or frozen for up to 2 months.

PREPARATION TIME 45 MINUTES (PLUS REFRIGERATION TIME)
COOKING TIME 35 MINUTES (PLUS COOLING TIME)

225g PLAIN FLOUR
110g SELF-RAISING FLOUR
50g CORNFLOUR
60g CUSTARD POWDER
185g CHILLED BUTTER, CHOPPED
1 TABLESPOON WHITE SUGAR
1 EGG, SEPARATED
80ml ICED WATER, APPROXIMATELY
2 TABLESPOONS APRICOT JAM
2 TEASPOONS WHITE SUGAR, EXTRA

FILLING
7 LARGE GREEN-SKINNED APPLES (1.5kg)
125ml WATER
55g WHITE SUGAR
½ TEASPOON GROUND CINNAMON
1 TEASPOON FINELY GRATED LEMON RIND

1 Make filling.
2 Sift flours and custard powder into large bowl; rub in butter, add sugar. Make well in centre, add egg yolk and enough of the water to mix to a firm dough; knead lightly. Cover; refrigerate 1 hour.
3 Preheat oven to moderately hot (200°C/180°C fan-assisted).
4 Roll out just over half of the pastry, on floured surface, until just large enough to line a 23cm (9in) pie plate. Lift pastry into pie plate; press into side, trim edge. Spread base of pastry with apricot jam, top with filling.
5 Roll out remaining pastry until large enough to cover pie. Brush edges of pie with a little lightly beaten egg white; cover with pastry. Press edges together firmly, trim and decorate. Brush pastry with egg white; sprinkle with extra sugar. Cut a few slits in pastry to allow steam to escape. Bake about 25 minutes or until golden brown.

FILLING Peel, quarter and core apples; cut each quarter in half lengthways. Combine apples in large saucepan with the water, sugar, cinnamon and rind. Bring to a boil, simmer, covered, about 5 minutes or until apples are almost tender. Remove from heat; drain, cool to room temperature.

SERVES 8

SUGAR

STORAGE Tart can be made a day ahead stored in an airtight container.
■ Tart is suitable for freezing.

bakewell tart

PREPARATION TIME 30 MINUTES (PLUS REFRIGERATION TIME)
COOKING TIME 25 MINUTES (PLUS COOLING TIME)

100g BUTTER
2 TABLESPOONS CASTER SUGAR
1 EGG YOLK
150g PLAIN FLOUR
60g GROUND ALMONDS
1½ TABLESPOONS RASPBERRY JAM
2 TABLESPOONS APRICOT JAM

FILLING
125g BUTTER
110g CASTER SUGAR
2 EGGS
90g GROUND ALMONDS
2 TABLESPOONS RICE FLOUR
½ TEASPOON GRATED LEMON RIND

LEMON ICING
55g ICING SUGAR
2 TEASPOONS LEMON JUICE

1 Cream butter, sugar and egg yolk in small bowl with electric mixer until combined. Stir in sifted flour and almonds in 2 batches. Knead dough on floured surface until smooth; cover, refrigerate 30 minutes.
2 Roll dough between sheets of baking parchment until large enough to line 24cm (9½in) flan tin. Lift pastry into tin, ease into side of tin; trim edge.
3 Spread base of pastry with raspberry jam; spread filling over jam.
4 Place tart on baking tray; bake in moderately hot oven 25 minutes or until lightly browned.
5 Place apricot jam in small pan; heat, strain. Brush top of hot tart with hot jam; cool. Pipe or drizzle lemon icing over tart.

FILLING Cream butter and sugar in small bowl with electric mixer until mixture is light and fluffy; beat in eggs 1 at a time. Stir in almonds, rice flour and rind.

LEMON ICING Sift icing sugar into small bowl, stir in juice; stir until smooth.

SERVES 8

BAKEWELL TART probably had its origins in Elizabethan times, but was made famous by a cook at the Rutland Arms in Bakewell, England, around 200 years ago.

STRUDEL (OPPOSITE PAGE) is usually considered German or Austrian in origin, but the strudel is also claimed by Hungary, where it is called *retes*. It probably came to all these areas from Turkey, as *baklava*.

apple strudel

PREPARATION TIME 30 MINUTES COOKING TIME 50 MINUTES (PLUS COOLING TIME)

5 LARGE APPLES (ABOUT 1kg)
65ml WATER
1 TEASPOON GRATED LEMON RIND
1 CLOVE
1/2 TEASPOON GROUND CINNAMON
1/2 TEASPOON GROUND NUTMEG
2 TABLESPOONS GROUND ALMONDS
75g WALNUTS, CHOPPED
150g SULTANAS
5 SHEETS FILO PASTRY
60g BUTTER, MELTED
2 TABLESPOONS GROUND ALMONDS, EXTRA
ICING SUGAR

1 Peel, core, quarter and thinly slice apples. Combine in pan with water, rind and clove, cover; cook about 10 minutes or until apples are tender. Discard clove; cool apple mixture.
2 Combine cold apple mixture in bowl with spices, nuts and sultanas.
3 Layer pastry sheets together, brushing each with butter and sprinkling with extra ground almonds. Spread filling to within 2cm (3/4in) of edge of a long side, leaving 5cm (2in) at each end. Fold ends in, roll up like a Swiss roll.
4 Place strudel on greased baking tray, brush with butter. Bake in moderate oven about 40 minutes or until lightly browned.
5 Dust strudel with sifted icing sugar before serving. Serve warm or cold with custard or cream.

SERVES 6

TIP Always keep filo covered while handling, as the thin sheets tend to dry out and break up.

STORAGE Strudel can be made a day ahead, stored covered, in refrigerator.

almond pear flan

PREPARATION TIME 30 MINUTES (PLUS REFRIGERATION TIME)
COOKING TIME 35 MINUTES

185g PLAIN FLOUR
90g CHILLED BUTTER, CHOPPED
55g CASTER SUGAR
2 EGG YOLKS
125g SOFTENED BUTTER, EXTRA
75g CASTER SUGAR, EXTRA
2 EGGS
1 TABLESPOON PLAIN FLOUR, EXTRA
120g GROUND ALMONDS
3 MEDIUM PEARS (690g), PEELED, CORED, QUARTERED
2 TABLESPOONS APRICOT JAM

1 Preheat oven to moderate (180°C/160°C fan-assisted).
2 Process flour, butter, sugar and egg yolks until combined. Transfer to lightly floured surface, knead into a smooth ball; cover, refrigerate pastry 30 minutes.
3 Beat extra butter and extra sugar until combined; beat in eggs and extra flour until combined. Stir in ground almonds.
4 Roll pastry to line 22cm (9in) round loose-based flan tin. Spread almond mixture into pastry case, top with pear. Bake about 35 minutes. Brush with warmed sieved jam.

SERVES 8

TIP You need about three lemons for this tart.

STORAGE Tart is best made a day ahead; keep, covered, in refrigerator.

lemon tart

PREPARATION TIME 30 MINUTES (PLUS REFRIGERATION TIME)
COOKING TIME 55 MINUTES

185g PLAIN FLOUR
55g ICING SUGAR
30g GROUND ALMONDS
125g CHILLED BUTTER, CHOPPED
1 EGG YOLK

LEMON FILLING
1 TABLESPOON FINELY GRATED LEMON RIND
125ml LEMON JUICE
5 EGGS
165g CASTER SUGAR
250ml WHIPPING CREAM

1 Blend or process flour, icing sugar, ground almonds and butter until combined. Add egg yolk, process until ingredients just come together. Knead dough on floured surface until smooth. Wrap in cling film, refrigerate 30 minutes.
2 Roll pastry between sheets of baking parchment until large enough to line 24cm (9½in) round loose-based flan tin. Lift pastry into tin; press into side, trim edge. Cover; refrigerate 30 minutes.
3 Meanwhile, preheat oven to moderately hot (200°C/180°C fan-assisted).
4 Place flan tin on baking tray. Line pastry case with baking parchment, fill with dried beans or rice. Bake, uncovered, 15 minutes. Remove parchment and beans; bake about 10 minutes or until browned lightly.
5 Meanwhile, whisk ingredients for lemon filling in medium bowl; stand 5 minutes.
6 Reduce oven temperature to moderate (180°C/160°C fan-assisted).
7 Pour lemon filling into pastry case; bake about 30 minutes or until filling has set slightly, cool.
8 Refrigerate until cold. Serve dusted with sifted icing sugar, if desired.

SERVES 8

BAKING BLIND
The method of cooking called 'baking blind' is used in this recipe. The pastry is placed into the tin but it is first cooked without any filling, weighted down with dried beans, peas or rice on baking parchment or greaseproof paper. Baking blind ensures a crisp pastry case, especially when using a 'wet' filling as with a quiche or a custard tart.

Placing dried beans in pastry cases

STORAGE This recipe is best made on the day of serving.

custard tarts

PREPARATION TIME 25 MINUTES (PLUS THAWING TIME)
COOKING TIME 30 MINUTES (PLUS COOLING TIME)

4 EGG YOLKS
110g CASTER SUGAR
2 TABLESPOONS CORNFLOUR
250ml CREAM
125ml WATER
STRIP OF LEMON RIND
2 TEASPOONS VANILLA ESSENCE
1 SHEET READY-ROLLED BUTTER PUFF PASTRY

1 Preheat oven to hot. Grease a 12-hole 80ml muffin tray. Place egg yolks, sugar and cornflour in medium saucepan; whisk until combined. Gradually whisk in cream and the water until smooth.
2 Add rind; stir over medium heat until mixture just comes to a boil. Remove from heat immediately. Remove rind; stir in essence.
3 Cut pastry sheet in half. Remove plastic; stack halves on top of each other. Stand about 5 minutes or until thawed. Roll pastry up tightly, from the short side; cut log into 12 x 1cm (½in) rounds.
4 Lay pastry, cut-side up, on lightly floured board; roll each round out to about 10cm (4in). Press rounds into prepared muffin trays with fingers. Spoon custard into pastry cases.
5 Bake tarts in hot oven about 20 minutes or until well browned. Transfer to wire rack to cool.

MAKES 12

treacle tart

This hearty and very old English recipe was once a feature of restaurant and cafe menus. Its American cousin is known as molasses pie.

PREPARATION TIME 30 MINUTES
(PLUS REFRIGERATION TIME)
COOKING TIME 25 MINUTES

190g PLAIN FLOUR
50g CUSTARD POWDER
2 TABLESPOONS ICING SUGAR
125g BUTTER, CHOPPED
2 TABLESPOONS MILK, APPROXIMATELY

FILLING
100g STALE BREADCRUMBS
345g TREACLE
2 TEASPOONS GRATED LEMON RIND

1 Sift flour, custard powder and icing sugar into medium bowl, rub in butter. Add enough milk to make ingredients cling together. Press dough into a ball; knead gently on floured surface until smooth. Cover; refrigerate 30 minutes.
2 Roll $^{2}/_{3}$ of the dough until large enough to line 22cm (9in) flan tin. Lift pastry into tin, gently ease into side; trim edge.
3 Place tin on baking tray, line pastry with baking parchment, fill with dried beans or rice. Bake in moderately hot oven 10 minutes. Remove paper and beans; bake further 10 minutes or until lightly browned, cool.
4 Spread filling into pastry case. Roll remaining pastry into a rectangle on floured surface; cut into 1cm (½in) strips. Brush edge of pastry case with a little extra milk. Place pastry strips over filling in lattice pattern; brush pastry with a little extra milk.
5 Bake in moderate oven about 25 minutes or until pastry is lightly browned. Cool tart in tin.
6 Sprinkle tart with a little icing sugar before serving. Serve with whipped cream or ice-cream.

FILLING Combine all ingredients in bowl; mix well.

SERVES 6 TO 8

STORAGE Treacle tart can be made a day ahead; store covered, in the refrigerator.
Treacle tart is suitable for freezing.

gourmet chocolate tart

PREPARATION TIME 40 MINUTES (PLUS REFRIGERATION TIME)
COOKING TIME 30 MINUTES

2 EGGS
2 EGG YOLKS
55g CASTER SUGAR
250g DARK EATING CHOCOLATE, MELTED
200g BUTTER, MELTED

TART SHELL
225g PLAIN FLOUR
110g CASTER SUGAR
140g CHILLED BUTTER, CHOPPED
1 EGG, BEATEN LIGHTLY

1 Make tart shell.
2 Reduce oven to moderate (180°C/160°C fan-assisted).
3 Whisk eggs, egg yolks and sugar in medium heatproof bowl over medium saucepan of simmering water about 15 minutes or until light and fluffy. Gently whisk chocolate and butter into egg mixture.
4 Pour mixture into tart shell. Bake, uncovered, in moderate oven about 10 minutes or until filling is set; cool 10 minutes. Refrigerate 1 hour. Serve dusted with sifted cocoa powder, if desired.

TART SHELL Blend or process flour, sugar and butter until crumbly; add egg, process until ingredients just come together. Knead dough on floured surface until smooth. Enclose in cling film; refrigerate 30 minutes. Grease 24cm (9½in) round loose-based flan tin. Roll dough between sheets of baking parchment until large enough to line prepared tin. Lift dough onto tin; press into side, trim edge, prick base all over with fork. Cover; refrigerate 30 minutes. Preheat oven to moderately hot (200°C/180°C fan-assisted). Place tin on baking tray; cover dough with baking parchment, fill with dried beans or rice. Bake, uncovered, in moderately hot oven 10 minutes. Remove paper and beans carefully from tin; bake, uncovered, in oven about 5 minutes or until tart shell browns lightly. Cool to room temperature.

SERVES 8

pear tart tatin

PREPARATION TIME 20 MINUTES (PLUS REFRIGERATION TIME)
COOKING TIME 1 HOUR 15 MINUTES

3 LARGE FIRM PEARS (990g)
90g BUTTER, CHOPPED
110g FIRMLY PACKED BROWN SUGAR
160ml CREAM
35g TOASTED PECANS, CHOPPED COARSELY

PASTRY
185g PLAIN FLOUR
55g ICING SUGAR
90g BUTTER, CHOPPED
1 EGG YOLK
1 TABLESPOON WATER

TATINS originated in France where they are a staple, classic dessert. For this recipe we have used pears, but you can substitute over-ripe bananas, classic apple (use golden delicious or sweet apples rather than cooking apples), quince (making sure to cook the fruit until thoroughly soft), or even prunes. Or make a savoury tatin using tomatoes and leaving out the sugar.

1 Peel and core pears; cut lengthways into quarters.
2 Melt butter with brown sugar in large frying pan. Add cream, stirring, until sugar dissolves; bring to a boil. Add pears; reduce heat, simmer, turning occasionally, about 45 minutes or until tender.
3 Meanwhile, make pastry.
4 Preheat oven to hot (220°C/200°C fan-assisted). Place pears, round-side down, in deep 22cm (9in) round cake tin; pour caramelised pan liquid over pears, sprinkle with nuts.
5 Roll pastry between sheets of baking parchment until slightly larger than circumference of prepared tin. Remove top paper, turn pastry onto pears. Remove remaining paper; tuck pastry between pear quarters and side of tin.
6 Bake, uncovered, in hot oven about 25 minutes or until pastry is lightly browned. Cool 5 minutes; turn tart onto plate, serve with whipped cream, if desired.

PASTRY Blend or process flour, icing sugar and butter until mixture is crumbly. Add egg yolk and the water; process until ingredients just come together. Enclose in cling film; refrigerate 30 minutes.

SERVES 6

sticky date pudding with butterscotch sauce

PREPARATION TIME 35 MINUTES COOKING TIME 1 HOUR 5 MINUTES

250g COARSELY CHOPPED STONED DATES
310ml WATER
1 TEASPOON BICARBONATE OF SODA
60g BUTTER
165g CASTER SUGAR
2 EGGS
150g SELF-RAISING FLOUR

BUTTERSCOTCH SAUCE
220g FIRMLY PACKED BROWN SUGAR
250ml CREAM
200g BUTTER

1 Preheat oven to moderate (180°C/160°C fan-assisted). Grease deep 20cm (8in) round cake tin; line base with baking parchment.
2 Combine dates and the water in medium saucepan, bring to a boil; remove from heat, add soda, stand 5 minutes. Blend or process mixture until smooth.
3 Beat butter, sugar and one of the eggs in small bowl with electric mixer until light and fluffy. Beat in remaining egg. (Mixture will curdle at this stage, but will come together later.) Stir in sifted flour then date mixture.
4 Pour mixture into pan; bake about 55 minutes. Stand pudding 10 minutes before turning onto wire rack over oven tray; turn pudding top-side up.
5 Meanwhile, make butterscotch sauce.
6 Pour 125ml sauce over pudding. Return pudding to moderate oven; bake, uncovered, further 5 minutes. Serve pudding with remaining sauce.

BUTTERSCOTCH SAUCE Combine ingredients in medium saucepan; stir over heat, without boiling, until sugar is dissolved. Simmer 3 minutes.

SERVES 6

STORAGE Pudding can be made four days ahead; keep, covered, in refrigerator. Reheat single servings in microwave oven on HIGH (100%) setting for about 30 seconds just before serving.

TIP It is important to have the apple mixture as hot as possible before topping with the sponge mixture. The heat from the apples starts the cooking process.

STORAGE Apple sponge is best made just before serving.

apple sponge

PREPARATION TIME 20 MINUTES
COOKING TIME 25 MINUTES

4 LARGE APPLES (ABOUT 800g)
55g CASTER SUGAR
65ml WATER

SPONGE TOPPING
2 EGGS
75g CASTER SUGAR
2 TABLESPOONS CORNFLOUR
2 TABLESPOONS PLAIN FLOUR
2 TABLESPOONS SELF-RAISING FLOUR

1 Peel, core, quarter and slice apples. Combine in pan with sugar and water, cover; cook about 10 minutes or until apples are tender.
2 Spoon hot apple mixture into deep 14cm (5½in) round ovenproof dish (1.5-litre capacity); spread sponge topping over mixture.
3 Bake in moderate oven about 25 minutes.

SPONGE TOPPING Beat eggs in small bowl with electric mixer about 7 minutes or until thick and creamy. Gradually add sugar, beating until dissolved after additions. Fold in sifted flours.

SERVES 4 TO 6

Originally an English pudding, this dish is sometimes called baked lemon pudding. There are now many variations of this delicious light pudding.

lemon delicious

PREPARATION TIME 20 MINUTES
COOKING TIME 50 MINUTES

3 EGGS, SEPARATED
110g CASTER SUGAR
30g BUTTER, MELTED
250ml MILK
2 TEASPOONS GRATED LEMON RIND
85ml LEMON JUICE
75g SELF-RAISING FLOUR
110g CASTER SUGAR, EXTRA

1 Beat egg yolks and sugar in small bowl with electric mixer until thick and creamy; transfer to large bowl. Stir in butter, milk, rind, juice and sifted flour.
2 Beat egg whites in small bowl with electric mixer until soft peaks form; add extra sugar gradually, beating until dissolved after additions. Fold into lemon mixture in 2 batches.
3 Pour mixture into lightly greased ovenproof dish (1.5-litre capacity), or 6 individual dishes (250ml capacity). Place in baking dish with enough hot water to come halfway up side of dish, or dishes.
4 Bake in moderate oven about 50 minutes (about 30 minutes for individual dishes) or until pudding is set.

SERVES 6

STORAGE Lemon delicious is best made just before serving.

STORAGE Pudding is best made just before serving.

chocolate self-saucing pudding

PREPARATION TIME 10 MINUTES COOKING TIME 40 MINUTES

150g SELF-RAISING FLOUR
1/2 TEASPOON BICARBONATE OF SODA
50g COCOA POWDER
275g FIRMLY PACKED BROWN SUGAR
80g BUTTER, MELTED
120g SOURED CREAM
1 EGG, BEATEN LIGHTLY
500ml BOILING WATER

1 Preheat oven to moderate (180°C/160°C fan-assisted). Grease deep 1.5-litre ovenproof dish.
2 Sift flour, soda, half of the cocoa and 100g of the sugar into medium bowl; stir in combined butter, sour cream and egg.
3 Spread mixture into prepared dish. Sift remaining cocoa and remaining sugar evenly over mixture; gently pour over the boiling water.
4 Bake, uncovered, in moderate oven about 40 minutes. Stand 5 minutes before serving. Serve with vanilla ice-cream, if desired.

SERVES 6

STORAGE Rice pudding can be made a day ahead; store covered, in the refrigerator.

rice pudding

This creamy pudding is perhaps the most loved and homely of British desserts.

PREPARATION TIME 10 MINUTES COOKING TIME 2 HOURS

100g SHORT-GRAIN RICE
625ml MILK
110g CASTER SUGAR
2 TABLESPOONS SULTANAS
1 TEASPOON VANILLA ESSENCE
2 TEASPOONS BUTTER
GROUND NUTMEG OR GROUND CINNAMON

1 Lightly grease shallow ovenproof dish (1-litre capacity).
2 Wash rice well under cold water; drain well. Combine rice, milk, sugar, sultanas and essence in prepared dish, mix lightly with a fork. Dot top with butter, sprinkle lightly with nutmeg.
3 Bake in moderately slow oven about 2 hours or until most of the milk has been absorbed.
4 Serve warm or cold with fruit, if desired.

SERVES 4

steamed jam puddings

PREPARATION TIME 15 MINUTES COOKING TIME 25 MINUTES

110g RASPBERRY JAM
1 EGG
110g CASTER SUGAR
150g SELF-RAISING FLOUR
125ml MILK
25g BUTTER, MELTED
1 TABLESPOON BOILING WATER
1 TEASPOON VANILLA EXTRACT

1 Preheat oven to moderate (180°C/160°C fan-assisted). Grease four 180ml metal moulds; divide jam among moulds.

2 Beat egg and sugar in small bowl with electric mixer until thick and creamy. Fold in sifted flour and milk, in two batches, then combined butter, water and extract.

3 Top jam with pudding mixture. Place moulds in medium baking dish; pour enough boiling water into dish to come halfway up sides of moulds. Bake, uncovered, about 25 minutes. Stand 5 minutes; turn onto serving plates. Serve puddings warm with vanilla custard or cream, if desired.

TIP You can use any flavour of jam for this recipe.

SERVES 4

Chocolate and prune are a texture and taste combination made in heaven. This cake has been prepared by being mixed in a food processor; some chocolate bits remain intact but they soften to melting point during baking.

hot chocolate prune cake

210g STONED PRUNES
310ml BOILING WATER
1 TEASPOON BICARBONATE OF SODA
60g BUTTER, CHOPPED
150g FIRMLY PACKED BROWN SUGAR
150g SELF-RAISING FLOUR
2 EGGS
100g DARK CHOCOLATE, CHOPPED COARSELY

CHOCOLATE SAUCE
300ml CREAM
120g DARK CHOCOLATE, CHOPPED COARSELY

Adding eggs to prune mixture

Chopping chocolate coarsely

PREPARATION TIME 15 MINUTES BAKING TIME 1 HOUR

1 Position oven shelves; preheat oven to moderate. Grease 20cm (8in) baba pan or ring mould thoroughly.
2 Combine prunes and the water in bowl of food processor; add soda, place lid of processor in position; stand 5 minutes.
3 Add butter and sugar to processor, pulse until ingredients are just combined.
4 Add flour then eggs; pulse until ingredients are just combined.
5 Add chocolate; pulse until chocolate is just mixed into mixture (pieces of chocolate will still be visible). Pour mixture into prepared baba pan or ring mould.
6 Bake cake in moderate oven about 1 hour. Stand cake 10 minutes then turn onto serving plate. Serve hot with chocolate sauce.

CHOCOLATE SAUCE Combine cream and chocolate in small saucepan; stir over low heat until chocolate is melted.

SERVES 8

TIPS This cake can also be made by the more conventional method: chop prunes, combine with the water and soda in a medium bowl, cover; stand 5 minutes. Using wooden spoon, stir in the finely chopped butter until melted then stir in sugar, lightly beaten eggs, flour and finely chopped chocolate. Follow baking directions above.

- It is important the baba pan be well greased, because the cake mixture is both very wet and very sugary (two conditions making it likely to stick to the pan when baked).
- Freeze serving-size pieces of cake, individually sealed in freezer bags, to have a ready-to-serve dessert on hand. Thaw each piece on HIGH (100%) in a microwave oven for about 30 seconds; serve hot with cream and/or ice-cream. The sauce can also be reheated quickly in your microwave oven.

STORAGE Cake will keep for up to 1 week in an airtight container at room temperature.

- Cake can be frozen for up to 3 months.

STORAGE Lemon meringue pots are best made just before serving.

MERINGUE Cooks and scientists argue about the egg whites. Some say they are best beaten at room temperature; others say to beat them at refrigerator temperature. We found eggs at both temperatures could be beaten satisfactorily to a good volume. If it is wet or humid, you are unlikely to get good results for meringues, due to their sugar content.
■ The whites should be very fresh and of good quality. Apparently, the diet of the hens and the time of year can also affect the egg whites. The best advice is to use large egg whites and to be very fastidious about dissolving every last grain of sugar.

warm lemon meringue pots

PREPARATION TIME 20 MINUTES COOKING TIME 15 MINUTES

2 TABLESPOONS CORNFLOUR
110g CASTER SUGAR
60ml LEMON JUICE
125ml WATER
1 TEASPOON FINELY GRATED LEMON RIND
2 EGGS, SEPARATED
30g BUTTER, CHOPPED
2 TABLESPOONS WHIPPING CREAM
75g CASTER SUGAR, EXTRA

1 Preheat oven to moderately hot.
2 Combine cornflour and sugar in small pan. Gradually add juice and water; stir until smooth. Cook, stirring constantly, until mixture boils and thickens. Reduce heat; simmer, stirring, 1 minute. Remove from heat; stir in rind, egg yolks, butter and cream.
3 Divide mixture between four 125ml ovenproof dishes. Place dishes on baking tray.
4 Beat egg whites in small bowl with electric mixer until soft peaks form. Gradually beat in extra caster sugar until dissolved.
5 Spoon meringue over filling. Bake in moderately hot oven about 5 minutes or until browned lightly. Serve with sponge finger biscuits, if desired.

SERVES 4

STORAGE These crumbles are best made just before serving.

apricot almond crumbles

PREPARATION TIME 15 MINUTES COOKING TIME 30 MINUTES

825g CAN APRICOT HALVES IN NATURAL JUICE
1 TABLESPOON BRANDY
75g SELF-RAISING FLOUR
¾ TEASPOON GROUND GINGER
30g GROUND ALMONDS
55g BROWN SUGAR
55g CASTER SUGAR
90g BUTTER, CHOPPED

1 Preheat oven to moderate (180°C/160°C fan-assisted).
2 Drain apricots over a small jug or bowl; reserve 125ml of the juice. Slice apricots and divide among six 180ml ovenproof dishes; place dishes on baking tray. Combine brandy with reserved juice; pour over apricots.
3 Sift flour and ginger into medium bowl; stir in almonds and sugars, then rub in butter with fingertips.
4 Sprinkle crumble mixture over fruit and bake in moderate oven about 30 minutes or until browned lightly. Serve hot with ice-cream or cream, if desired.

SERVES 6

crème brulée

PREPARATION TIME 15 MINUTES (PLUS REFRIGERATION TIME)
COOKING TIME 40 MINUTES

1 VANILLA POD
750ml WHIPPING CREAM
6 EGG YOLKS
55g CASTER SUGAR
55g ICING SUGAR, APPROXIMATELY

1 Preheat oven to moderately low. Split vanilla pod in half lengthways. Using the point of a sharp knife, scrape seeds from bean; reserve seeds. Place pod and cream in medium saucepan; heat until just below boiling point.
2 Meanwhile, whisk egg yolks, caster sugar and vanilla seeds in medium heatproof bowl; gradually whisk in hot cream mixture. Place bowl over medium saucepan of simmering water – do not let the water touch the base of the bowl. Stir over heat about 10 minutes or until mixture thickens slightly and coats the back of a spoon.
3 Remove pod – it can be washed, dried and kept for another use. Place six 125ml ovenproof dishes in baking dish; pour cream mixture into ovenproof dishes level with the top as they will shrink slightly. Add enough boiling water to baking dish to come ¾ of the way up side of dishes. Bake in moderately low oven about 20 minutes or until custard is just set. Remove dishes from water; cool to room temperature. Cover; refrigerate 3 hours or overnight.
4 Place dishes in shallow baking dish filled with ice-cubes (the ice helps to keep custard firm while grilling). Sprinkle each custard evenly with a heaped teaspoon of sifted icing sugar; wipe edge of dishes. Place under hot grill until sugar is just melted, not coloured. Sprinkle custards again with a second layer of sifted icing sugar; place under hot grill until sugar is golden brown.

SERVES 6

■ CUSTARD is simply a combination of milk, eggs, sugar and flavouring (usually vanilla). You can make a stirred custard as a sauce for desserts, or bake the mixture to form a set custard. Stirred custard is best cooked over simmering water whereas a set custard is usually baked by placing the dish in a water bath or bain marie; water prevents the mixture from becoming too hot and curdling.

■ You can use custard to make crème caramel, bread and butter pudding, rice custard and trifle, as well as countless other delicious desserts.

TIPS Alternatively, use a small cook's blow torch to melt and caramelise the sugar.

STORAGE This recipe can be prepared a day ahead; grill the tops up to an hour before serving.

STORAGE Baked apples best made just before serving.
- Baked custard can be made a day ahead; store covered, in refrigerator.

baked apples

Granny Smith and Golden Delicious apples are the best varieties to use for baking.

PREPARATION TIME 10 MINUTES COOKING TIME 45 MINUTES

4 MEDIUM APPLES (ABOUT 600g)
50g BUTTER, SOFTENED
65g BROWN SUGAR
100g SULTANAS
1 TEASPOON GROUND CINNAMON

1 Remove cores from apples, cut 1cm (½in) from base of each core, push back into base of each apple to act as a plug. Slit skin of each apple around the centre.
2 Beat butter and sugar in small bowl until smooth, stir in sultanas and cinnamon. Fill apple cavities with creamed sugar mixture.
3 Stand apples in greased ovenproof dish. Bake, uncovered, in moderate oven about 45 minutes or until apples are tender; brush occasionally with pan syrup during cooking.

SERVES 4

baked custard

Don't aerate the custard by whisking the eggs too much. Its texture when cooked should be creamy smooth.

PREPARATION TIME 15 MINUTES COOKING TIME 45 MINUTES

6 EGGS
2 TEASPOONS VANILLA ESSENCE
75g CASTER SUGAR
1 LITRE HOT MILK
GROUND NUTMEG

1 Whisk eggs, essence and sugar together in bowl. Gradually whisk milk into egg mixture, pour into lightly greased ovenproof dish (1.5-litre capacity), sprinkle with nutmeg.
2 Stand ovenproof dish in baking dish with enough boiling water to come halfway up side of ovenproof dish.
3 Bake, uncovered, in moderate oven about 45 minutes or until custard is firm.

SERVES 6

baked apples (left)
baked custard (right)

STORAGE Pancakes are best made just before serving.
■ Pancakes suitable for freezing.

pancakes

PREPARATION TIME 10 MINUTES (PLUS STANDING TIME)
COOKING TIME 10 MINUTES

300g PLAIN FLOUR
4 EGGS, LIGHTLY BEATEN
500ml MILK
BUTTER
60ml LEMON JUICE, APPROXIMATELY
2 TABLESPOONS SUGAR, APPROXIMATELY

1 Sift flour into bowl, gradually add combined eggs and milk; mix, or blend or process, until mixture is smooth. Cover; stand 30 minutes.
2 Lightly grease heated heavy-based pan with butter; pour about 3 tablespoons batter evenly into pan. Cook pancake until lightly browned underneath; turn, cook until lightly browned.
3 Keep pancakes warm while cooking remaining batter. Serve the pancakes sprinkled with lemon juice and sugar.

MAKES ABOUT 15

■ Historians think that pancakes, in the form of grain meal and water cooked on hot stones, were the first recipe invented by primitive cooks. Almost every culture has a version, from France's crepes to Mexico's tortillas.
■ Pancakes are great eaten hot, sprinkled with sugar and lemon or lime juice. The good thing about them is that they are easy to make, can be frozen, layered with cling film between them, and can be used as a basis for sweet and savoury recipes.
■ An almost flat pan with a heavy base measuring about 20cm (8in) is ideal for cooking pancakes. Some cooks keep a pan for this use only – once it has been seasoned by use, there is no need to wash it; just wipe dry with a pad of kitchen paper.

Pouring batter into centre of pan

Flipping pancake using spatula

TIPS Substitute any dried fruit of your choice in this recipe. If the dried fruit is hard, chop and then soak in a little boiling water about 30 minutes or until it is soft; drain well before using.

STORAGE Recipe can be made a day ahead; store covered, in refrigerator.

Bread and butter pudding is an old English favourite, originally devised to use up stale bread. The bread needs to be a little dry for best results.

bread & butter pudding

PREPARATION TIME 15 MINUTES (PLUS STANDING TIME)
COOKING TIME 50 MINUTES

6 THIN SLICES WHITE BREAD
40g BUTTER
3 EGGS
55g CASTER SUGAR
625ml MILK
1 TEASPOON VANILLA ESSENCE
100g SULTANAS
GROUND NUTMEG OR GROUND CINNAMON

1 Trim crusts from bread, butter each slice; cut into 4 triangles. Arrange 2 rows of triangles, butter-side up, overlapping slightly, along base of shallow ovenproof dish (2-litre capacity). Centre another row of triangles over first 2 rows, with triangles facing in opposite direction to triangles in first layer.
2 Whisk eggs, sugar, milk and essence together in bowl.
3 Pour ½ the custard mixture over bread; stand 10 minutes.
4 Whisk remaining custard mixture again, add sultanas; pour into dish. Sprinkle with nutmeg or cinnamon. Stand dish in baking dish, with enough boiling water to come halfway up side of dish.
5 Bake, uncovered, in moderately slow oven about 50 minutes or until custard is set. Serve hot or cold with stewed or canned fruit and cream.

SERVES 4 TO 6

TIPS Cream mixture suitable to microwave.

STORAGE Recipe should be made a day ahead; store covered, in refrigerator for up to 4 days.

hazelnut crème caramel

PREPARATION TIME 25 MINUTES (PLUS STANDING AND REFRIGERATION TIMES) COOKING TIME 55 MINUTES

- 125g HAZELNUTS
- 250ml MILK
- 375ml CREAM
- 165g CASTER SUGAR
- 180ml WATER
- 3 EGGS
- 3 EGG YOLKS
- 110g CASTER SUGAR, EXTRA

1 Preheat oven to moderate. Place nuts in shallow baking tin; bake in moderate oven about 8 minutes or until skins begin to split and nuts are toasted lightly. Place nuts in tea towel; rub vigorously to remove skins. Chop nuts coarsely. Reduce oven temperature to low.

2 Bring milk, cream and nuts to a boil in medium saucepan; cover. Remove from heat; stand 20 minutes.

3 Meanwhile, combine sugar and the water in medium saucepan; stir over low heat, without boiling, until sugar dissolves. Brush down side of pan with pastry brush dipped in water to remove any sugar grains. Bring to a boil; boil, uncovered, without stirring, until mixture is caramel in colour. Remove from heat; divide between six 180ml ovenproof moulds. The toffee will set immediately.

4 Combine eggs, egg yolks and extra sugar in medium bowl; whisk until just combined. Bring milk and cream back to a boil; gradually whisk into egg mixture until combined. Strain mixture into large jug; discard nuts.

5 Pour custard over toffee in moulds; place moulds into baking dish. Pour enough boiling water into baking dish to come ¾ of the way up side of moulds.

6 Bake, uncovered, in slow oven 35 minutes. Custards are ready when only the centre has a slight wobble to it. Remove from baking dish; refrigerate at least 8 hours or overnight. The refrigeration time allows the toffee to dissolve, which forms the sauce.

7 Gently pull custard away from side of moulds. Invert onto serving plates.

SERVES 6

Brushing sugar crystals from side of pan

Boiling sugar mixture rapidly

COOKING CRÈME CARAMEL

Crème caramel is a rich, classic dessert; it is spectacular in appearance and taste, yet is simple to make.

- It is important to add boiling water to the baking dish in which the pot of crème caramel is to be cooked. This is called a water bath or bain marie, and prevents the temperature of the food from rising too high while it is in the oven. If crème caramel was not cooked in a water bath, it would probably reach boiling point and would curdle.
- Remember to remove the dessert from water in baking dish, or custard will continue to cook and may curdle.
- It is also important to allow crème caramel to come to room temperature before refrigerating it overnight.

STORAGE Cheesecake can be made a day ahead; keep, covered, in refrigerator.

lemon cheesecake

PREPARATION TIME 30 MINUTES (PLUS REFRIGERATION TIME)

250g PACKET PLAIN SWEET BISCUITS
125g BUTTER, MELTED
250g PACKET CREAM CHEESE, SOFTENED
395g CAN SWEETENED CONDENSED MILK
2 TEASPOONS FINELY GRATED LEMON RIND
80ml LEMON JUICE
1 TEASPOON GELATINE
1 TABLESPOON WATER

1 Blend or process biscuits until mixture resembles fine breadcrumbs. Add butter; process until combined. Press biscuit mixture evenly over base and side of 20cm (8in) springform tin, place on tray; refrigerate about 30 minutes or until firm.
2 Meanwhile, beat cream cheese in small bowl with electric mixer until smooth. Beat in condensed milk, rind and juice; beat until smooth.
3 Sprinkle gelatine over the water in small heatproof jug; stand jug in small saucepan of simmering water. Stir until gelatine dissolves; cool 5 minutes.
4 Stir gelatine mixture into lemon mixture. Pour mixture into crumb crust; cover cheesecake; refrigerate about 3 hours or until set.

SERVES 8

The essence of a mousse is lightness, indicated by its French name, which means foam or froth. This chocolate version is delicate yet rich.

Adding sugar to egg whites at soft peak stage

Folding egg white mixture into chocolate mixture

chocolate mousse

PREPARATION TIME 15 MINUTES (PLUS REFRIGERATION TIME)
COOKING TIME 10 MINUTES

200g DARK CHOCOLATE, CHOPPED
30g UNSALTED BUTTER
3 EGGS, SEPARATED
300ml CARTON WHIPPING CREAM, WHIPPED

1 Place chocolate in heatproof bowl, place over pan of simmering water; stir chocolate until melted, remove from heat. Add butter, stir until melted; stir in egg yolks one at a time. Transfer mixture to large bowl, cover; cool.

2 Beat egg whites in small bowl with electric mixer until soft peaks form. Fold the cream and egg whites into chocolate mixture in 2 batches.

3 Pour into 12 serving dishes (85-ml capacity); refrigerate several hours or overnight.

4 Serve with extra whipped cream and chocolate curls, if desired.

SERVES 12

STORAGE Recipe best made a day ahead; store covered, in refrigerator.

This cake is almost a cross between a mousse and a fallen soufflé. It's an impressive cake to present for dessert or with tea and coffee, but it must be made on the day of serving. This recipe does not contain flour.

200g DARK CHOCOLATE, CHOPPED COARSELY
60mL HOT WATER
1 TEASPOON INSTANT COFFEE POWDER
4 EGGS, SEPARATED
110g CASTER SUGAR
1 TABLESPOON CASTER SUGAR, EXTRA
125ml WHIPPING CREAM
1 TABLESPOON KIRSCH

CHERRY FILLING
425g CAN PITTED BLACK CHERRIES
3 TEASPOONS CORNFLOUR
1 TABLESPOON KIRSCH

Folding egg whites into chocolate mixture

Rolling cake

black forest roulade

PREPARATION TIME 20 MINUTES BAKING TIME 10 MINUTES

1 Position oven shelves; preheat oven to moderate. Grease 25cm x 30cm (10in x 12in) Swiss roll tin; line base with baking parchment.
2 Combine chocolate, water and coffee in large heatproof bowl; sit bowl over pan of simmering water. Using wooden spoon, stir until chocolate melts then immediately remove bowl from pan to bench.
3 Beat egg yolks and sugar in small bowl with electric mixer until thick and creamy; this will take about 5 minutes. Using large metal spoon, fold egg mixture into warm chocolate mixture.
4 Beat egg whites in small bowl with electric mixer until soft peaks form. Using metal spoon, gently fold egg whites into chocolate mixture, in two batches. Spread mixture into prepared tin. Bake in moderate oven about 10 minutes.
5 Meanwhile, place large sheet of baking parchment on board; sprinkle with extra sugar. Turn cake onto sugared baking parchment; carefully remove lining paper, cover cake loosely with tea-towel. Cool cake to room temperature.
6 Beat cream and kirsch in small bowl with rotary or electric mixer until firm peaks form. Spread cake evenly with cooled cherry filling then spread kirsch cream over cherry mixture. Roll cake from a long side, using paper to lift and guide the roll; place on serving plate. Cover roll; refrigerate 30 minutes before serving.

CHERRY FILLING Drain cherries, reserving 60ml of syrup. Using knife, chop cherries coarsely. Using wooden spoon, blend cornflour and reserved syrup in small saucepan. Add cherries; stir over heat until mixture boils and thickens. Remove from heat, stir in kirsch; cover surface of mixture with plastic wrap, cool to room temperature.

SERVES 6

TIPS To successfully make this cake, it is vital that the egg yolk/sugar mixture is beaten until thick and that the egg whites are beaten only to soft peaks. Overbeating will dry out the whites and make it difficult to fold them into the chocolate mixture.
■ We used a large metal spoon for the folding process; a plastic spatula also works well.
■ To test if this cake is cooked, touch it with your fingertips: it should feel slightly firm and springy.

STORAGE Cake will keep for up to 8 hours in an airtight container in the refrigerator. Unrolled and unfilled cake can be stored, covered with a piece of baking paper then a damp tea-towel, overnight in the refrigerator.

STORAGE Recipe best made a day ahead; store covered, in refrigerator.

TRIFLE is always a winner with all age groups, and is a luscious way to dress up plain cake with jelly, custard, fruit and cream. You can vary the ingredients to suit yourself or whatever you have on hand.

■ We like the method of setting the cake in jelly as a base, but some people prefer to place the cake in the bowl, sprinkle it with orange juice or sherry, then add jelly and custard, nuts and fruit, according to the texture and flavour required.

■ The custard can be made over direct heat (not over water) because it contains custard powder and can withstand boiling. However, a custard using eggs as a thickening agent should be made in a double saucepan.

trifle

PREPARATION TIME 25 MINUTES (PLUS REFRIGERATION AND STANDING TIME)
COOKING TIME 10 MINUTES

100g PACKET STRAWBERRY JELLY CRYSTALS
300g JAM SWISS ROLL
65ml SHERRY
425g CAN SLICED PEACHES, DRAINED
300ml WHIPPING CREAM, WHIPPED

CUSTARD
2 TABLESPOONS CUSTARD POWDER
2 TABLESPOONS CASTER SUGAR
500ml MILK
1 TEASPOON VANILLA ESSENCE

1 Make jelly according to packet directions; refrigerate until jelly is just beginning to set.

2 Cut sponge roll into 1cm (½in) slices, place over base and around side of large glass serving bowl; sprinkle with sherry. Pour partly set jelly over sponge roll; refrigerate until jelly is set.

3 Place peaches over jelly, spread evenly with custard, top with cream; refrigerate. Serve with fresh fruit, if desired.

CUSTARD Blend custard powder and sugar with a little of the milk in pan, stir in remaining milk. Stir over heat until custard boils and thickens. Remove from heat, stir in essence; cover; cool.

SERVES 6 TO 8

STORAGE Recipe can be made a day ahead; store covered, in refrigerator.

syllabub

In Elizabethan England, frothing milk was mixed with wine or cider to create this dish.

125ml DRY WHITE WINE
2 TEASPOONS GRATED LEMON RIND
2 TABLESPOONS LEMON JUICE
110g CASTER SUGAR
300ml CARTON WHIPPING CREAM
250g PUNNET STRAWBERRIES, SLICED

PREPARATION TIME 15 MINUTES (PLUS REFRIGERATION TIME)

1 Combine wine, rind, juice and sugar in small bowl; stir until sugar is dissolved. Add cream; beat with electric mixer until it forms soft peaks.
2 Divide berries between 6 glasses. Serve syllabub over berries; refrigerate 2 hours before serving. Serve syllabub with extra berries and lemon rind, if desired.

SERVES 6

glossary

ALLSPICE also known as pimento; tastes like a blend of cinnamon, clove and nutmeg.

ALMONDS

Flaked sliced almonds.

Ground we use packaged commercially ground nuts, unless otherwise specified.

Slivered almonds cut lengthwise.

ARROWROOT used mostly for thickening; cornflour can be substituted.

BAKING POWDER a raising agent consisting mainly of 2 parts cream of tartar to 1 part bicarbonate of soda (baking soda).

BICARBONATE OF SODA also known as baking soda.

BISCUIT CRUMBS, sweet use any plain, sweet biscuits (cookies). Blend or process biscuits until finely and evenly crushed.

BREADCRUMBS

Packaged fine-textured, purchased white breadcrumbs.

Stale 1- or 2-day-old white bread made into crumbs by blending or processing.

BUTTER use salted or unsalted (also called sweet) butter.

BUTTERMILK low-fat milk cultured with bacteria to give a slightly sour, tangy taste; low-fat yogurt can be substituted.

CHEESE

Cream also known as 'Philadelphia' or 'Philly'; a soft milk cheese having no less than 33% butterfat.

Ricotta a fresh, unripened cheese made from whey.

CHOCOLATE

Dark we used a good-quality cooking chocolate.

Chocolate chips also known as chocolate chips and chocolate morsels; small buds of dark chocolate, made of cocoa liquor, cocoa butter, sugar and an emulsifier, that hold their shape in baking.

COCOA cocoa powder.

COCONUT we used desiccated coconut unless otherwise specified.

Essence extract.

Flaked flaked and dried coconut flesh.

Shredded thin strips of dried coconut flesh.

COLOURINGS many types are available from cake decorating suppliers, craft shops and supermarkets; all are concentrated. Use a minute amount of any type of colouring first to determine its strength.

liquid the strength varies depending on the quality; useful for colouring most types of icings where pastel colours are needed. Large amounts of liquid colourings will dilute or break down most icings.

powdered these are edible and are used when primary colours or black are needed.

concentrated pastes these are a little more expensive but are the easiest to use; are suitable for both pastel and stronger colours.

CORN SYRUP available in light or dark colours. Glucose syrup can be substituted.

CORNFLOUR also known as cornstarch; used as a thickening agent in cooking.

CORNMEAL ground, dried corn (maize); similar to polenta but slightly coarser. One can be substituted for the other but textures will vary.

CREAM

fresh also known as pure cream and pouring cream; has no additives like commercially thickened cream (minimum fat content 35%).

Sour a thick, commercially cultured soured cream (minimum fat content 35%).

Sour Light a less dense, commercially cultured soured cream; do not use this instead of sour cream.

Whipping a cream (minimum fat content 35%) containing a thickener such as gelatine.

CUSTARD POWDER packaged powdered mixture of starch (wheat or corn), artificial flavouring and colouring.

DATES fruits of the date palm tree, thought to have originated in North Africa, with a thick, sticky texture and sweet mild flavour. Sometimes sold stoned and chopped; can be eaten fresh or dried on their own, or cooked to release their flavour.

ESSENCE also known as extract. Usually the by-product of distillation of plants.

FLOUR

plain all-purpose flour, made from wheat.

self-raising substitute plain flour and baking powder in the proportion of 112g of plain flour to 2 teaspoons of baking powder; sift together several times before using. If using an 8oz measuring cup, use 1 cup of plain flour to 2 teaspoons of baking powder.

Rice flour made from rice; ground rice can be substituted.

GELATINE we used powdered gelatine.

GINGER

Glace fresh ginger root preserved in sugar syrup. Crystallised ginger can be substituted if rinsed with warm water and dried well before using.

Ground also known as powdered ginger; cannot be substituted for fresh ginger.

GLUCOSE SYRUP (liquid glucose) clear syrup with a consistency like honey; it is made from wheat starch. Available at health food stores and supermarkets. Do not confuse it with the powdered glucose drink.

GOLDEN SYRUP a by-product of refined sugarcane; pure maple syrup or honey can be substituted.

GRAND MARNIER an orange-flavoured liqueur.

GROUND RICE rice flour can be substituted, although it will give a finer texture than ground rice.

HAZELNUTS, GROUND we used packaged commercially ground nuts.

JAM also known as preserve or conserve; most often made from fruit.

JELLY CRYSTALS fruit-flavoured gelatine crystals available from supermarkets.

KIRSCH a cherry-flavoured liqueur.

LIQUEURS we have used a variety of liqueurs; if desired, you can use brandy instead (but the flavour will change). If alcohol is not desirable, substitute fruit juice of an equivalent flavour or milk or water to balance the liquid proportions in the recipe.

MAPLE SYRUP distilled sap of the maple tree.

MARSALA a sweet fortified wine.

MARZIPAN a smooth, firm confectionery paste.

MILK we used full-cream homogenised milk unless otherwise specified.

Evaporated unsweetened canned milk from which water has been extracted.

Sweetened condensed a canned milk product consisting of milk with more than half the water content removed and sugar added to the milk that remains.

MIXED DRIED FRUIT a combination of sultanas, raisins, currants, mixed peel and cherries.

MIXED PEEL a mixture of crystallised citrus peel; also known as candied peel.

MIXED SPICE a blend of ground spices, usually consisting of cinnamon, allspice and nutmeg.

OIL we used polyunsaturated vegetable oil unless otherwise specified.

PUFF PASTRY, READY-ROLLED frozen sheets of puff pastry available from supermarkets.

PUNNET small basket usually holding about 250g fruit.

RIND zest.

RUM, DARK we used an underproof (not overproof) rum for a more subtle flavour.

SUGAR we used coarse granulated table sugar (also known as crystal sugar) unless otherwise specified.

Brown an extremely soft finely granulated sugar retaining molasses for its deep colour and flavour.

Caster also known as superfine or finely granulated table sugar.

Demerara small golden-coloured crystal sugar.

Icing also known as confectioners' sugar or powdered sugar.

SULTANAS seedless white raisins.

TREACLE thick, dark syrup not unlike molasses; a by-product of sugar refining. Golden syrup or honey can be substituted.

VANILLA POD dried long thin pod of vanilla orchid. The minuscule black seeds inside the bean are used to impart a vanilla flavour in baking and desserts. One bean can be used repeatedly; simply wash in warm water after use, dry well and store in airtight container.

VANILLA ESSENCE we used imitation vanilla extract.

WINE we used good-quality dry white and red wines.

index

WARNING This book contains recipes for dishes made with raw or lightly cooked eggs. These should be avoided by vulnerable people such as pregnant and nursing mothers, invalids, the elderly, babies and young children.

conversion charts

MEASURES

- The spoon measurements used in this book are metric: one metric tablespoon holds 20ml; one metric teaspoon holds 5ml.
- All spoon measurements are level.
- The most accurate way of measuring dry ingredients is to weigh them.
- When measuring liquids, use a clear glass or plastic jug with metric markings.
- We use large eggs with an average weight of 60g.

DRY MEASURES

metric	imperial
15g	1/2oz
30g	1oz
60g	2oz
90g	3oz
125g	4oz (1/4lb)
155g	5oz
185g	6oz
220g	7oz
250g	8oz (1/2lb)
280g	9oz
315g	10oz
345g	11oz
375g	12oz (3/4lb)
410g	13oz
440g	14oz
470g	15oz
500g	16oz (1lb)
750g	24oz (1 1/2lb)
1kg	32oz (2lb)

LIQUID MEASURES

metric	imperial
30ml	1 fl oz
60ml	2 fl oz
100ml	3 fl oz
125ml	4 fl oz
150ml	5 fl oz (1/4 pint/1 gill)
190ml	6 fl oz
250ml	8 fl oz
300ml	10 fl oz (1/2 pt)
500ml	16 fl oz
600ml	20 fl oz (1 pint)
1000ml (1 litre)	1 3/4 pints

LENGTH MEASURES

metric	imperial
3mm	1/8in
6mm	1/4in
1cm	1/2in
2cm	3/4in
2.5cm	1in
5cm	2in
6cm	2 1/2in
8cm	3in
10cm	4in
13cm	5in
15cm	6in
18cm	7in
20cm	8in
23cm	9in
25cm	10in
28cm	11in
30cm	12in (1ft)

OVEN TEMPERATURES

These oven temperatures are only a guide for conventional ovens. For fan-assisted ovens, check the manufacturer's manual.

	°C (Celcius)	°F (Fahrenheit)	gas mark
Very low	120	250	1/2
Low	150	275-300	1-2
Moderately low	170	325	3
Moderate	180	350-375	4-5
Moderately hot	200	400	6
Hot	220	425-450	7-8
Very hot	240	475	9